From the library of

SOPHENE

HAGOP BARONIAN

BALTHAZAR!
A COMEDY IN THREE ACTS

TRANSLATED BY
KIMBERLEY MCFARLANE &
BEYON MILOYAN

SOPHENE BOOKS
LOS ANGELES

Published by Sophene 2022

Copyright © Kimberley McFarlane and Beyon Miloyan 2022

All Rights Reserved. No part of this publication may be reproduced in any form or by any means without the written permission of the publisher.

Balthazar! was first published in 1886 in Constantinople in the Western dialect of the Armenian language. This translation was made from the original issues of *Khikar* in which *Balthazar!* was originally published.

www.sophenebooks.com
www.sophenearmenianlibrary.com

ISBN-13: 978-1-925937-81-7

BALTHAZAR!

First published in 1886 and long considered as one of Baronian's masterpieces, *Balthazar!* presents a farcical insight into the trials and tribulations of marital life in Constantinople's Armenian upper-class. When Balthazar discovers that his wife, Anush, has been seen with another man, he hires a lawyer to initiate a divorce and appeals to his best friend Gibar to discover her lover's identity. Unbeknownst to the foolish Balthazar, the adulterer is none other than Gibar himself who, determined to protect Anush's reputation, engages in a conspiracy to frame Balthazar in a competing case. What ensues is an outrageous tribunal with tragicomic results.

Hagop Baronian is regarded as one of the finest Armenian satirists and playwrights. Born to a modest family in Adrianople in 1843, Baronian attended two academies, where, in addition to Armenian and Turkish, he learned Italian, French, Bulgarian, and Greek. In 1863, he moved to Constantinople where he worked in various jobs to help his family financially. A voracious reader of classical and European literature, he got his literary start in 1872 working as editor-in-chief for the Constantinople-based Armenian periodical, *Euphrates*, and spent the next two decades of his life writing. Baronian earned numerous enemies and censors in his lifetime for shedding light not only on the corruption of Ottoman officials, but also on the depravity of Constantinople's large Armenian population, sparing no one from wealthy nobles and Armenian clergy all the way down to the lower classes. Though he was widely known and his works were widely read in his day, he died in abject poverty, leaving behind his wife and two young children. His works went on to be hugely influential in the 20th century and today he holds a place among Armenia's most renowned literary figures.

Translators' Note

> *"The Satyre should be like the Porcupine,*
> *That shoots sharpe quils out in each angry line"*
>
> —*Joseph Hall*

Widely considered as one of Baronian's masterpieces, *Balthazar!* was originally serialized in seven issues of the Armenian monthly, *Khikar,* in 1886-87. Baronian composed his work in the Western Armenian dialect with elements of formal, Classical Armenian style as well as contemporary slang from the mouths of different characters. In our translation we have strived for a faithful reproduction of the work, having afforded ourselves some license to translate unique Western Armenian expressions and phrases into corresponding English phrases from the period. We hope our translation captures as much of the enjoyment, humor, and dare we say, even offense, as it did for countless readers and viewers over the course of the 19th and 20th centuries.

    Kimberley McFarlane
    Beyon Miloyan

Characters

Balthazar, *Anush's husband*

Anush ("sweet"), *Balthazar's wife*

Gibar ("cypress"), *Anush's lover*

Oksen ("Auxentius"), *lawyer*

Pailag ("lightning")
Yergat ("iron") } *Magistrates*
Soor ("sword")

Takuhi ("queen")
Martha } *Balthazar's neighbors*

Salome, *Balthazar's maid*

ACT I

Scene presents a large room sumptuously furnished. Two doors on the left and two on the right. Windows look out to the street and garden. A door in the center.

Scene I

ANUSH *(sitting at the window facing the street with a handkerchief in her hand)*, **GIBAR**, *then* **SALOME**

GIBAR. My dear! It is time to work, not to cry. Wipe your tears and listen to me for a moment.

ANUSH. *(Wiping her tears.)* Do you promise to protect me, then?

GIBAR. If I thought for a moment of abandoning or leaving you – you, whom I have adored for ten years and will worship forever – I would be doing a most cowardly deed. Be calm, I am going to use all my skills to thwart your husband's devices; I am going to make him despair and even apologize to you.

ANUSH. He is not one to despair so easily, especially as he is more stubborn than usual; he will use all his efforts to defame me... Oh! My dearest Gibar, the only thing that pains me is the delicate point of being accused of immorality before the tribunal and—

GIBAR. I do not perceive even a glimmer of immorality. God forbid! What, have you robbed orphans of their rights?

Have you extorted other people's inheritances? Have you committed theft? Homicide? Not at all! Far from it! You simply do not love your husband and love me instead. Is this not your only fault (if this could even be considered a fault)?

ANUSH. Yes! I have loved you, only you!

GIBAR. And how could you have loved a man like ol' Balthazar? An unattractive, unintelligent, unseemly man, who is anything *but* a man, and with whom you have nothing in common. You would have done a horrible injustice to logic, public opinion, taste, feelings, and nature itself if you thought that you had been born for ol' Balthazar. No, no, my dear! Those blue eyes of yours may grow faint as long as they burn, but they will never extinguish. Those eyes were not made for the pleasures and desires of a boorish man like ol' Balthazar! Nature has destined you for me, but accident has given you to Balthazar. He is a rapacious thief who has snatched you, but you, you belong to me. He is worthy of a hanging, that instead of marrying a woman who corresponds to his sentiments, and a woman suitable to himself, he dared to snatch you, who shines bright like a jewel in high society.

ANUSH. Oh! Your words restore my spirits a little, my dear Gibar.

GIBAR. Rest assured. You are innocent and your cause is pure. Be strong! Do as I say and don't be afraid. I am going to play such tricks on him that he will regret everything he has done.

ANUSH. Yes, let's shame him!

GIBAR. Let him consult all the lawyers in the world; he will not be able to establish any grounds. His entire proof amounts to seeing you coming out of a questionable house. That is a weak argument to get rid of a woman... the case is very delicate.

ANUSH. Even though I have subjected myself to my own rebellious feelings by loving you, even though I know it's impossible to resist the heart's currents, and even though I am persuaded that I am innocent in this affair, I still want everyone to think that I never loved you and that I've always been faithful to my husband.

GIBAR. Of course. We are going to try to convict him of slander.

ANUSH. And if we are unsuccessful...

GIBAR. We will absolutely succeed! It is enough for you to follow my instructions.

ANUSH. I promise.

GIBAR. Here are my instructions then. First—

ANUSH. *(Looking out the window and seeing her husband coming.)* He is coming, I must leave.

GIBAR. Go! We'll see each other later, or I will send my instructions with Salome.

SALOME. Hurry, go! He's moving quickly... **(ANUSH** *departs.)* You should have advised and consoled her earlier, so she wouldn't get so emotional.

GIBAR. She'll adjust.

SALOME. You should have seen the poor woman last night. It was unbearable... she cried for hours, and your ol' Balthazar turned into a raging bull. He was fuming... if there was only some cause for it! My God. What need is there to rage, for the love of God? Was his dinner not ready? Were his clothes not washed? Was his bed not made? Come home, sit down, enjoy your dinner, and go to bed! But no, ol' Balthazar has always been critical... he fumes over every trivial thing.

GIBAR. All because of his nit-picking...

Scene II

GIBAR and BALTHAZAR

BALTHAZAR. *(Entering quickly.)* They call me Balthy... *(To* **SALOME.***)* Get out! And close the door, do not allow anyone to enter! Quick, quick! Get out, quickly... *(To* **GIBAR.***)* Forgive me, Mr. Gibar, for sending for you. When a man meets adversity, he naturally goes to his closest friends for advice. Tremendous misfortune has befallen me—since last night, I have felt as though I'm losing my mind. I don't know what I'm doing or what I'm saying. I have a family secret to tell you—you, my only friend, whom I completely trust.

GIBAR. Thank you, that is most noble of you.

BALTHAZAR. I don't reveal my secrets to everybody, and though from all appearances I may seem coarse and idiotic, by God's mercy I recognize my enemies and my friends. I am in charge of my affairs, that's why they call me Balthy!

GIBAR. Yes.

BALTHAZAR. I trust you'll keep the secret I'm about to tell you.

GIBAR. Of course.

BALTHAZAR. So I don't need to beg you not to tell anyone my secret.

GIBAR. No need.

BALTHAZAR. My secret is...... my wife has a lover.

GIBAR. *(In a loud voice.)* Your wife has a lover?!

BALTHAZAR. Don't yell! Salome will hear, and I don't want Salome to know my family secrets. Speak softer.

GIBAR. You said your wife has a lover? Ah... that is unbelievable!

BALTHAZAR. It is believable, my dear friend, it is believable.

GIBAR. How long has she had this lover?

BALTHAZAR. Only a few weeks, I think. Would I let my wife have a lover for a long time? I would know immediately. Take a good look at me. Do you think I'm an idiot, like other husbands? Do you think some debauched man would make love to my wife, and I wouldn't find out? How clever you are...

GIBAR. Who is this philanderer, then?

BALTHAZAR. I want to know who the philanderer is, too— that scoundrel, that snake in the grass, that wretch, who brought ruin to my house. That's why I beg you to help me find the scoundrel. You can coax his name from my wife. Go to her and try to lure the name of the scoundrel.

GIBAR. Very well.

BALTHAZAR. Actually, I've already sent a man to that evil and scandalous house that my most modest wife came out of yesterday.

GIBAR. You don't say...

BALTHAZAR. I told you, they don't call me Balthy for no reason. Yes, I sent someone there to investigate who the man was with Mrs. Anush yesterday.

GIBAR. *(Aside.)* Our case is under way, but if they've found me out, things could change.

BALTHAZAR. What do you think?

GIBAR. Nothing. *(Aside.)* If they have found me out...

BALTHAZAR. Go, quickly! Go to that room and try to discover the first and last names of that scoundrel. But don't tell my wife that I've also resorted to other means to identify her lover. Hurry, go—find out and come back. Let me open my case against these two scoundrels today, so they understand that it's not so easy to tarnish the honor of a man like me.

GIBAR. All right, goodbye for now. *(Aside.)* But first, let's get our own affairs in order... *(Departs.)*

Scene III

BALTHAZAR, *then* **OKSEN** *and* **SALOME**

BALTHAZAR. Look at how he goes running to look after my affairs. A man who would give up his soul for me—a good, modest, noble, and dependable man, the likes of which is hard to find these days...

SALOME. *(From outside.)* I won't let you in.

OKSEN. *(From outside.)* I'm coming in.

BALTHAZAR. That's Oksen... I forgot...

SALOME. *(From outside.)* No!

OKSEN. *(From outside.)* Yes! (He pushes the door open and enters.) What an offense this is, ol' Balthazar!

BALTHAZAR. Forgive me! I'm losing my mind...

OKSEN. Balthazar, why offend me like this?

BALTHAZAR. It's my fault...

OKSEN. What insult, what dishonor, what hostility is this, ol' Balthazar? You invite me to your house, then order your maid not to let me in!

BALTHAZAR. I forgot...

OKSEN. What did you forget?

BALTHAZAR. To give the order...

OKSEN. What do you mean "to give the order"?

BALTHAZAR. To allow you.

OKSEN. What does "to allow you" mean? What does "to allow you" have to do with my question? To allow you, he says...

BALTHAZAR. To allow you to come inside.

OKSEN. Nonsense. Empty words, worthless excuses. This is a serious case. A lawyer, an attorney, a justice of the peace is violated, insulted, dishonored—I demand satisfaction and compensation. You know the law imposes a fine of twenty liras on a person convicted of such an offense? Correspondingly, you and your servant will each pay twenty liras.

SALOME. I beg you, I—

OKSEN. No.

BALTHAZAR. Most honorable sir—I beg you, forgive me, my head is not in the right place—

OKSEN. No.

SALOME. I misunderstood.

BALTHAZAR. It wasn't you who I told her not to admit.

SALOME. I thought you were a stranger.

BALTHAZAR. Why would we close our doors on you?

SALOME. You are always welcome, come any time.

BALTHAZAR. Most eminent sir, I beg your pardon, my home is ruined...

SALOME. Don't be angry... let me bring you some sweets.

BALTHAZAR. Bring coffee, bring brandy, bring wine, bring cognac.

OKSEN. I don't want anything. Let this be a lesson to you to avoid such indecent conduct another time. If it had been another attorney in my place, he would have immediately opened suit against you. But I forgive you because I see that there was a misunderstanding here. *(To* **SALOME.***)* Leave the room.

BALTHAZAR. *(To* **SALOME.***)* Leave the room! No, come here... I order you now: The doors of my house are to always remain open for Mr. Oksen, who is free to come to my house morning or evening, day or night.

SALOME. There's no need to order me.

BALTHAZAR. *(Aside.)* We've dodged a bullet.

SALOME. *(Aside.)* Curse you both.

Scene IV

BALTHAZAR *and* **OKSEN**

OKSEN. Let's turn to our case. How did you happen to get married to this woman? I need this information to firmly grasp the core of the situation.

BALTHAZAR. I met her when I went to the theater one night with a friend... I wish my legs had been broken, so I couldn't have gone! During the first act, the doors of the neighboring box opened, and a young woman entered with a young man... I wish they'd never come in! As soon as I saw the girl, I was attracted to her, and was gradually captivated by her beauty, her movements, the sound of her voice, and especially her laugh. So, I asked my friend if he knew her... I should have never asked! My friend said he knew her, that she was an orphan, and that she was a sweet, kind, humble, prudent, sensible, civilized, and educated girl, and that whoever married her would be doing a good deed by saving her from poverty. A few days later, I approached my relatives and a few friends for their opinions... I should have never approached them! They all said I had found a rare treasure, and I should possess that treasure without losing time. On this basis, I immediately proposed. In one week, we were engaged; and three days later, we were married.

OKSEN. So how does a woman with such a good reputation tumble into immorality?

BALTHAZAR. What do I care how she tumbled in? I want only to maintain the honor of my house and kick out that shameless woman, who I will never accept as a spouse. I insist that she get a fitting punishment.

OKSEN. Please, don't get so emotional. This case is delicate, we must think with cool heads and understand the legal disposition.

BALTHAZAR. Put her in an asylum,[1] chain her, starve her, beat her every night, break her bones, and remove such a shameless and dishonorable woman from the world!

---

[1] *P'rgich* ("Savior"), an Armenian hospital established in Constantinople in 1834 (still functional), which contained a psychiatric unit.

OKSEN. Watch your tongue. You have no right to call that woman shameless and dishonorable without a legal verdict. Your wife is still decent and respectable before the world and the law.

BALTHAZAR. Decent...? Respectable...? A woman seen leaving a disreputable house...

OKSEN. Did she enter the house by breaking down the door, or did she enter seeing that the doors were open?

BALTHAZAR. What does it matter? It's enough that she went inside.

OKSEN. It matters to me in this circumstance. Pray, tell me.

BALTHAZAR. Lord have mercy... how should I know? But there would have been no need to break down the door.

OKSEN. So, she found the door open and entered. A-ha! A mitigating factor, see?

BALTHAZAR. What? What's a mitigating factor?

OKSEN. It's a circumstance that mitigates a crime or lessens it.

BALTHAZAR. And then? What do they do with this lesser crime?

OKSEN. The punishment for a lesser crime is a lesser sentence.

BALTHAZAR. I don't understand the difference between this lesser or greater crime.

OKSEN. In legal terms, it's called a mitigating factor.

BALTHAZAR. I don't understand.

OKSEN. In French, it's *circonstances atténuantes*.

BALTHAZAR. I don't follow.

OKSEN. In Italian, it's *circostanze estenuanti*.

BALTHAZAR. I don't know Italian.

OKSEN. In German, it's *milderungsgründe*.

BALTHAZAR. Explain it differently.

OKSEN. In Greek, it's *elafryntikés peristáseis*.

BALTHAZAR. I know this *peristáseis*... I've heard it a lot! But I don't remember what it means.

OKSEN. In English, it's extenuating circumstances.

BALTHAZAR. Explain this stupid thing in Armenian.

OKSEN. An extenuating circumstance is a condition or circumstance that mitigates, lightens, reduces, or diminishes one's offense. It is a mitigating circumstance or justifiable reason that the guilty party seeks to lighten or lessen their punishment.

BALTHAZAR. Well, when you put it that way, I understand.

OKSEN. If your wife had entered by breaking the door, her punishment would have been heavier.

BALTHAZAR. I know. But she *did* enter that damned house to make love to someone.

OKSEN. But did she *intentionally* enter *specifically* to make love to someone, or did she just happen to make love?

BALTHAZAR. This has nothing to do with the honor of my house.

OKSEN. Was her lover a young man or an adult?

BALTHAZAR. Who knows? He can go to hell.

OKSEN. Is he handsome or ugly?

BALTHAZAR. Please, stop the interrogation.

OKSEN. Did she make love with good or evil intentions?

BALTHAZAR. How could a woman cheat on her husband with good intentions? What humiliation is this? Damn these mitigating factors and whoever invented them. My wife, my companion, my spouse, my partner has made love to someone else! She has committed a crime and a felony and is worthy of hanging.

OKSEN. You are in too much of a hurry to sentence her. Wait for the law to do an investigation, examine the case, and assess all the causes that made your wife take a lover. Maybe she has rights to love another. Leave it to me to examine the issue, so that we don't lose the case. You want your wife to be immediately punished based on your testimony. That is not possible. Many men like you, thinking themselves innocent, have opened suit against their wives, and have themselves been found guilty and culpable by tribunal.

BALTHAZAR. So according to you, my wife is innocent.

OKSEN. According to me, everything is obscure. I don't say that your wife is innocent, nor do I say she is guilty. I can neither excuse nor condemn the lover of your wife, nor do I dare say that you are the guilty one.

BALTHAZAR. Is there any possibility that I will be found guilty in this case?

OKSEN. Anything is possible.

BALTHAZAR. That means it won't be possible to put that woman in the asylum today.

OKSEN. That's impossible. The extenuating circumstances may be so advanced that if your wife has loved another with good intentions, as in to aid the progress and enlightenment of the nation, or for the benefit of orphans, the handicapped, the aged, the disabled, or to shelter the poor and the destitute for a praiseworthy enterprise that stands to benefit the nation, your wife will appear in the papers and receive praises and laurels, I mean for having had the heroism to sacrifice her own good name for the common good, and in this case—

BALTHAZAR. So I'm the guilty one...

OKSEN. On the contrary, if she made love to an ugly or old man, naturally this would increase her sentence. The law aside, public opinion would condemn her, saying, "Couldn't her lover at least have been a handsome young man or a sympathetic person?"

BALTHAZAR. Could we put her in the asylum tomorrow?

OKSEN. It's impossible. If you have given her a reason to have a lover by being unfaithful or jealous, or by your severe conduct toward her, you would be assuming great liability.

BALTHAZAR. I was mad about her. I never so much as looked at another woman!

OKSEN. Then rest assured. Time is money, I must go. I will use all my legal powers to present you as innocent in this case and to make your wife guilty.

BALTHAZAR. Don't take these "extenuating circumstances" of yours too seriously.

OKSEN. My duty will be to destroy the "extenuating circumstances" with strong and solid evidence.

BALTHAZAR. Thank you.

OKSEN. 'Til next time. *(Departs.)*

Scene V

BALTHAZAR

BALTHAZAR. Farewell "extenuating" lawyer! It wasn't going to be long until our Most Honorable Lawyer was going to make *me* out to be guilty. If I'd been a blabbermouth and an idiot, there's no doubt he would have wanted to make me out to be the guilty one and excuse the actual perpetrator. That debauched woman would have turned into an innocent dove because she has this "extenuating circumstance," he says, and because this "extenuation" is also in French, Italian, Greek, German, and English, he says; because she did not cheat with loving intentions, he says, but she happened to make love incidentally, he says; because she didn't love him with evil intentions, he says, but with good intentions, he says. She loved him as an act of charity, he says, because... how should I know why?! There is no end to these "becauses"! And all these "becauses" are proving the innocence of that unfaithful woman, mind you—that shameless, unfaithful woman and hellish creature. What a clever mind you have, master attorney! Well, we also know a little something about lawyering. We, too, have read the catechism back in the day. We do not gulp down these "extenuating" stories so easily. My father was like this, too, God bless his soul. Many went to him for advice. My grandfather was intelligent, too. Our whole lineage was like this. We are lawyers by nature and immediately understand who has the right in such situations...

Scene VI

BALTHAZAR *and* ANUSH

ANUSH. I cannot stand your insults any longer—
BALTHAZAR. Yet you still dare show your face in front of me?

ANUSH. —and I want us to separate immediately.

BALTHAZAR. If you had even a little shame, you would go to your room and pull your hair out and—

ANUSH. Why should I pull my hair out? I should rub perfumes on my hair for being saved from an ungrateful man like you. What a pity, ten thousand pities, that I brought you into high society! When you married me, you didn't even know how to give a proper greeting. I rue my efforts to knock some sense into you and dress you like a man! I rue those pains I took to teach you how to dance! When you married me, you didn't even know how to walk straight. Pity! Pity my sacrifices! It was after you married me that you came to know people. Before that, you looked like a cook with your baggy pants and long coat, and everyone would call you ol' Balthazar; but now that you have become somewhat of a gentleman, I have become shameless and disgraceful, is that right?

BALTHAZAR. I am of ungrateful stock...

ANUSH. A woman like me was too much for you; I knew you wouldn't be able to handle me because you hadn't grasped the spirit of the enlightenment of our age, and you regarded wives as slaves. I knew all this, but I endured, cursing the day I promised to marry you.

BALTHAZAR. I wish you hadn't...

ANUSH. My neighbors tried to persuade me not to marry you. They would say, "How are you going to live with someone as thick as a piece of wood?" And I would respond that my fiancé was a good man.

BALTHAZAR. I wish I wasn't...

ANUSH. How many people asked me after my marriage, "How do you spend time with that ass?" And I defended you then, telling them my husband was an intelligent man.

BALTHAZAR. All those people are the asses... and you're not even ashamed to make such disgraceful comments...

ANUSH. I'll never forget the day one of your friends told me, "I don't want to hurt your feelings—Balthazar is a good man, but he's very crass. It's impossible to talk to him." I came home and sat and cried for two hours. And some, not knowing that I was your wife—because there is no one who regarded you as suitable for me—would slander you and make fun of the things you did; and hearing them, I would be ashamed to reveal that I was your wife. What was I to do? I would bury it in my heart, cry, and not tell you a thing. I persisted in trying to make a man out of you and introducing you to society, and all my efforts were forgotten in one minute. Wonderful, just wonderful.

BALTHAZAR. And you did all this only to love another man?

ANUSH. Whom do I love?

BALTHAZAR. You know better than I do.

ANUSH. Jealousy has baffled your judgment; you like to imagine that I came out of a disreputable house.

BALTHAZAR. I saw it with my own eyes.

ANUSH. Then you consulted attorneys about how to let me go and make a mockery of me before the world, as if to defend your violated honor.

BALTHAZAR. I should have separated from you long ago, and now I'm going to use every means at my disposal to do it.

ANUSH. I have already resolved not to accept you as my husband, to separate from you entirely and never speak your name again.

Scene VII

Same and **GIBAR**

GIBAR. I would consider myself fortunate if I could intervene and bring about reconciliation between you—
BALTHAZAR. It's impossible.
ANUSH. Unfeasible.
GIBAR. —and to prevent an unfortunate separation.
ANUSH. I feel nothing but hatred toward him.
BALTHAZAR. She's more repulsive to me than the devil.
GIBAR. Listen, please.
ANUSH. Don't even try, I beg you.
BALTHAZAR. Don't get involved in this.
GIBAR. These things can happen in a marriage. Prudence demands that—
BALTHAZAR. The guilty one be punished.
ANUSH. Yes, I also demand that the guilty one be punished, and I want you to understand that a wife is not a slave. Let's suppose for a moment that I really have a lover, and that my having a lover was made public—what is one to do? Turn everything topsy-turvy? Take recourse to lawyers? Scream? Shout?
BALTHAZAR. Yes, yes!

GIBAR. You ought to call on your wife first—
ANUSH. Talk to her with a cool head—
GIBAR. Verify things with her—
ANUSH. Without getting angry—
GIBAR. And if she really has a lover—
ANUSH. Forgive and advise her—
GIBAR. So that another time—
ANUSH. She wouldn't make the same mistake—
GIBAR. And if she was caught a second time—
ANUSH. Forgive her again—
GIBAR. Advise and exhort her—
ANUSH. And tell her it is not a good thing—
GIBAR. To have a lover—
ANUSH. That leads her to have other lovers, too—
GIBAR. And that having many lovers—
ANUSH. Does not seem very pleasant to husbands—
GIBAR. And finally, to edify—
ANUSH. By exhorting—
GIBAR. Persuading—
ANUSH. Admonishing—
GIBAR. Rebuking—
ANUSH. Caressing—
GIBAR. Threatening—
ANUSH. Forgiving—
GIBAR. He should preserve the honor of the family—
ANUSH. And *this* is how to preserve the honor of a family—
GIBAR. As is done all over the world—
ANUSH. As we have seen from our fathers and mothers—
GIBAR. And not—
ANUSH. To get inflamed—
GIBAR. To recourse to lawyers—

ANUSH. To consult them—
GIBAR. To demand separation—
ANUSH. To be dishonored in court—
GIBAR. To be the talk of the town—
ANUSH. To be wrapped around a finger—
GIBAR. To lose friends—
ANUSH. To shut the doors of the house—
GIBAR. To ruin a family—
ANUSH. And then regret it—
GIBAR. And say 'I want my wife—'

> (**ANUSH** *and* **GIBAR** *speak so fast and snatch sentences from each other's mouths so quickly that* **BALTHAZAR**, *standing between them in bewilderment, can't find a chance to talk.*)

ANUSH. And fail to get her back—
GIBAR. And cry—
ANUSH. And wail—
GIBAR. And weep—
ANUSH. And sigh—
GIBAR. And lament—
ANUSH. And mourn—
GIBAR. How many more I could mention—
ANUSH. How many more I could reckon—
GIBAR. To feel pain and anguish—
ANUSH. To be burdened with sorrow—
GIBAR. To think, to ponder—
ANUSH. To spend time worrying—
GIBAR. To lose appetite—
ANUSH. To lose sleep—

GIBAR. To cough—

ANUSH. To moan—

GIBAR. And at last—

ANUSH. To die—

GIBAR. Isn't this what ought to be done?

ANUSH. I'm speaking in vain… this man cannot be persuaded.

BALTHAZAR. I am not the type of husband who forgives.

GIBAR. *(In **BALTHAZAR**'s ear.)* I couldn't get any secrets from her.

ANUSH. Please, don't oblige him to make amends because I have sworn never to love him.

BALTHAZAR. *(In a low voice to **GIBAR**.)* Keep trying to figure out the name of her lover. *(Aloud.)* Reconciliation is impossible. I have no time to listen to empty talk. I am going to find my lawyer and bring this case to the magistrates' tribunal. *(Departs.)*

Scene VIII

GIBAR *and* ANUSH

GIBAR. He has resolved to go ahead with his plans. The idiot thinks that by applying to the magistrates' court he will have them do what he wants. He will regret it later, but what use is that? He's only going to wear us down a little. Not to fear, it's enough that we work in harmony and remain loyal to each other. There is no doubt that he will sever ties with me when he finds out that we were both at Baidzar's house on the same day. Let him cut ties with me; it will be an opportunity to have more intimate ties with you.

ANUSH. Can we not win his lawyer over to our side?

GIBAR. Most lawyers find justice only where there is plenty of money to be made, though I'm not sure this applies to Oksen. If I succeed in coming to an agreement with him, good. If not, I will take it upon myself to defend your cause and continue to play our games. You can at least be sure that public opinion is going to be favorable to us.

ANUSH. I am extremely thankful, my dear, for your promise to courageously defend me. Your sacrifice doubles my love for you.

SCENE IX

Same and **OKSEN**

OKSEN. You are very audacious, Madam, to keep the person who disturbs your calm right beside you, even when you are about to be summoned to court with an indictment as being unfaithful to your husband. Instead of trying to find means to justify yourself, you are looking for proofs to confirm the crime you committed. The audacity!

GIBAR. She doesn't need to justify herself because she's not at fault.

OKSEN. And you still dare to continue your impudence after effectively destroying a family?

GIBAR. You are taking this too far.

OKSEN. On the contrary, I am not taking this far enough. You are more at fault than she is because you have scandalized her, and that is why you'll be sentenced with a much heavier punishment than she will.

GIBAR. *(Laughing.)* Please, have some pity, Mr. Lawyer...

OKSEN. Are you mocking me? You will be the only one punished, and I will work to make it so that the mistress here has no fault. I am going to make the case such that all the guilt falls on you, and you will be condemned to ten years of imprisonment.

GIBAR. Oh, poor me! *(Laughing.)* How about just four years instead?

OKSEN. Please go out and leave me alone with my client's wife.

GIBAR. No!

OKSEN. My client's wife is as good as my wife. Now get out!

GIBAR. She is my heart and soul. I would get jealous.

OKSEN. There is no need for your confession; your guilt has already been proven and confirmed. Get out and don't make me resort to severe measures.

GIBAR. No!

ANUSH. Please, don't fight over me.

OKSEN. It is absolutely necessary for him to get out. My duty as a lawyer demands that I be alone with you for a few minutes.

GIBAR. And my dignity demands that you not be alone with her at all.

OKSEN. Why are you so obstinate?

Scene X

Same and **BALTHAZAR**

BALTHAZAR. *(Urgently.)* What? What is it?

OKSEN. Yes, a private interview is necessary!

GIBAR. A private interview is completely unnecessary.

BALTHAZAR. *(To* **GIBAR**.*)* He is an attorney, don't talk to him like that.

GIBAR. *(Pushing* **BALTHAZAR**.*)* Don't meddle, this case has taken a new turn.

OKSEN. She is my client's wife, why don't you let me talk to her for two minutes?

BALTHAZAR. *(To* **OKSEN**.*)* He is a friend of ours — don't offend him.

OKSEN. *(Pushing* **BALTHAZAR**.*)* You started this case, now don't meddle in this. (To **GIBAR**.) Are you going to go out, because if not—

BALTHAZAR. *(To* **GIBAR**.*)* Go out for a bit, let's see what he's going to do.

GIBAR. *(Pushing* **BALTHAZAR**.*)* I'm not going to leave at all. I order you to leave.

OKSEN. I will notify the appropriate party of this.

GIBAR. Goodbye.

*(***BALTHAZAR** *tries to make peace between* **GIBAR** *and* **OKSEN***, running back and forth between the two, but is pushed away by both of them at the end of the scene).*

OKSEN. You will get due and proper treatment.

GIBAR. Get out of my sight.

OKSEN. Naturally, then, the consequences won't be favorable to you.

GIBAR. Good grief, I'm supposed to leave my friend's wife alone with our most honorable attorney...

OKSEN. My intentions are good... *(To* **BALTHAZAR**, *who was forcefully pulling his arm.)* Get out of here! For the love of God, why do you keep sticking your nose into this case? Let me talk.

GIBAR. Let him do his job, his lawyerly obligation supposedly demands a private interview that is supposedly necessary with his client's wife. *(To* **BALTHAZAR**, *who is trying to cover* **GIBAR***'s mouth with his hand.)* Why do you keep meddling in this, what is it to you? We will fight and we will reconcile... is anyone addressing you? Mind your own business.

BALTHAZAR. They won't let me talk... I'm going to burst...

OKSEN. *(To* **BALTHAZAR**.*)* Didn't you hire me to handle your case?

BALTHAZAR. Yes!

OKSEN. And your wife?

BALTHAZAR. Yes!

OKSEN. Then go mind your own business and don't meddle in the affairs of your representative.

BALTHAZAR. But— **(ANUSH** *and* **GIBAR** *depart.)*

OKSEN. Very well, but know that you will be punished cruelly, Mr. Gibar. *(Yelling through the door.)* You'll get twelve years in prison! And then...?! And then?! We'll see about that, too.

Scene XI

BALTHAZAR and OKSEN

BALTHAZAR. I came running, out of breath, to hear the important revelations that you have to tell me, but I couldn't get out of the fight to—

OKSEN. *(Talking to himself.)* You are useless, you wait, I'll teach you how to behave with a lawyer.

BALTHAZAR. Those important revelations...

OKSEN. You are senseless. You don't want to leave me alone with Anush? Don't then! You'll see...

BALTHAZAR. Are you going to make these important revelations?

OKSEN. *(Turning to the door.)* Shameless. I am an honorable man, I would not have stooped so low as to even talk to you. *(Suddenly bolting to the door and yelling.)* You are good for nothing! Who do you think I am, not letting me interview Mrs. Anush a little? You think I'm dishonorable like you—you, who are having a secret affair with your good friend's wife? Scandalizing the poor woman, seducing and misleading her, taking her out to someone else's house and drinking for hours, singing and dancing. You think I'm like you? You shameless son of a—you coward!

BALTHAZAR. His anger hasn't subsided enough for him to make these important revelations.

OKSEN. You slither like a snake into every home, and whenever you leave a home, its dignity and happiness depart with you. You frauds, you traitors!

BALTHAZAR. I beg you, that's enough. These important revelations...

OKSEN. If I had the authority, I would have you youngsters arrested and annihilated. How can a creature like you have any honor, a creature like you who has been making love to your friend Balthazar's wife for ten years—for ten years!

BALTHAZAR. Balthazar's...? What's this I hear? For ten years!

OKSEN. You found an idiot and you played him however you wanted, you fraud.

BALTHAZAR. Oh, it's another Balthazar... I thought for a second it was me and—

OKSEN. If I were in ol' Balthazar's shoes, I would tear you to pieces.

BALTHAZAR. Wait, he said ol' Balthazar... I don't understand...

OKSEN. It's not hard to deceive someone who is as mentally deficient and dried up as him. Come and fool me, if you can. You son of a—you vermin!

BALTHAZAR. Who could this ol' Balthazar be? Good grief, what an ass he must be...

OKSEN. But I am going to have the law condemn you to the most severe punishment as a criminal, and I will try to redeem Mrs. Anush.

BALTHAZAR. *(Yelling.)* Enough, Mr. Attorney! Enough! Come here, so we understand each other. Tell me about these important revelations.

OKSEN. What revelations? Everything has already been revealed! The lover of your wife is Gibar.

BALTHAZAR. You said Gibar?

OKSEN. Yes, Gibar! But remain calm, I am going to thrash everything he has done out of him. I have had a grudge with him for a long time already, and I never liked his conduct. The opportunity has presented itself to spill all my legal venom upon him to get my revenge. Come on then, let's get to work. First and foremost, we must decide on compensation for my future efforts. We lawyers customarily receive our payments in three parts: the first when we start working on the case, the second in the middle of the proceedings, and the third when the case is settled.

BALTHAZAR. You said it was Gibar?

OKSEN. So, you are obliged to pay fifty liras first, another fifty liras in the middle, and fifty liras at the end, for a total of one hundred and fifty liras, which is a trifling sum for separating from an unfaithful wife. I hope you will come out innocent from court, and that your opponents will receive a suitable punishment. But if, despite all my efforts, we are unable to achieve our desired outcome, I retain the right charge the full one hundred and fifty liras, because work is work.

BALTHAZAR. So that I don't misunderstand, you said Gibar, right?

OKSEN. Yes, G, I spells GI; B, A, R spells BAR: that's GI – BAR.

BALTHAZAR. Oh, you son of a—! Who would've thought... and he has been her lover for ten years? Good grief!

OKSEN. Yes!

BALTHAZAR. Who would believe it?

OKSEN. What is your response to my proposal?

BALTHAZAR. What can I say... bravo, Gibar, bravo...

OKSEN. You should say whether we will begin the proceedings or not.

BALTHAZAR. Bravo, Gibar! Well done!

OKSEN. One hundred and fifty liras isn't a large sum for separating from an unfaithful wife and a bad friend.

BALTHAZAR. One can get three wives with that sum, brother.

OKSEN. You're right, to let go of a wife is more expensive than to acquire one.

BALTHAZAR. Are you sure we will win this case, at least?

OKSEN. I am very sure. They do not have any extenuating circumstances.

BALTHAZAR. Good. It is enough to separate from that devil of a wife.

OKSEN. Hurry then and make the first payment, so we can complete our preparations. As you know, these preparations take a little while. First, the petition must be given to the president, who sends it to the Initiative Court; the Initiative Court sends it to the Competency Court; the Competency Court sends it to the Relations Council; the Relations Council sends it to the Editorial Council; the Editorial Council sends it to the Jurisdiction Council; the Jurisdiction Council to the Economic Council; the Economic Council to the Educational Council; from where it goes to the magistrates, who form a committee to examine the case. They then form a sub-committee to examine and report on the case, and this sub-committee will also resort to auxiliary divisions for help. The auxiliary divisions will have their branches examine all the particulars of the case, and each of these branches will have their sub-branches examine it; then, after their examinations, they report back to their branches, who report back to the auxiliary divisions, the auxiliary divisions report to the sub-divisions, the sub-divisions report to the sub-committee, and the sub-committee reports back to the committee, and thus the case returns to where it started. Then it goes back to the magistrates, who will judge the case. Let's go!

BALTHAZAR. What a long journey this is!

END OF ACT I

ACT II

Same setting as in Act I. To the right, a table with a heavy, green tablecloth, and a small bell, inkstand, paper, and pen on top.

Scene I

BALTHAZAR then OKSEN

BALTHAZAR. 'My wife has been found unfaithful in her marital duty. Her unfaithfulness has been established. Naturally then, it is necessary for us to separate, and, by law, for you to allow me to get another wife. My wife has been found unfaithful in her marital duty. Her unfaithfulness has been established. Naturally then, it is necessary for us to separate, and, by law, for you to allow me to get another wife.' Yes, this is what I will say to the magistrates—not a word more, not a word less: 'My wife has been found unfaithful in her marital duty. Her unfaithfulness has been established. Naturally then, it is necessary for us to separate, and, by law, for you to allow me to get another wife...'

OKSEN. *(Entering.)* I saw the magistrates; they are on their way now. Have you learnt your lines well?

BALTHAZAR. Smooth as water. 'My wife has been found unfaithful—'

OKSEN. Good. You are to act according to my advice.

BALTHAZAR. Yes!

OKSEN. Do not stray a hair from the path I showed you.

BALTHAZAR. No!

OKSEN. Only in this way can we win.

BALTHAZAR. Of course.

OKSEN. If you try some other way, you will lose the case.

BALTHAZAR. No doubt.

OKSEN. The magistrates will badger you with wall-to-wall questions to trap you. You will answer their questions only with the responses I have taught you.

BALTHAZAR. Yes! 'My wife has been found unfaithful in her marital duty. Her unfaithfulness has been established. Naturally then, it is necessary for us to separate, and, by law, for you to allow me to get another wife.'

OKSEN. Bravo!

BALTHAZAR. I will honor the magistrates, so they investigate my case favorably. Coffee, tea, sweets, brandy, sherbet...

OKSEN. I think they're coming. They're here.

Scene II

Same and **PAILAG, YERGAT,** *and* **SOOR**
(at the door)

PAILAG. *(To* **YERGAT.***)* Go ahead, please.

YERGAT. *(To* **SOOR.***)* Please, go ahead.

SOOR. *(To* **PAILAG.***)* You first.

PAILAG. It wouldn't be right for me to enter before you.

YERGAT. *(To* **PAILAG.***)* The rules of decency demand that I enter last.

SOOR. *(To* **YERGAT.***)* Never, we will not accept it.

PAILAG. *(To* **SOOR.***)* So why don't you lead the way?

SOOR. *(To* **PAILAG.***)* Unacceptable, you are preeminent.

PAILAG. *(To* **SOOR.***)* Your courteousness is what makes you think that way.

SOOR. *(To* **PAILAG.***)* And your courteous sentiments make you reason that way.

PAILAG. *(To* **SOOR.***)* Your sympathy makes you speak this way.

SOOR. *(To* **PAILAG.***)* It is the delicate nature of your sentiments—

YERGAT. *(To* **SOOR.***)* Let us not waste time; enter, please!

SOOR. *(To* **YERGAT.***)* You enter.

YERGAT. No, let the Honorable Soor enter!

SOOR. No! Let the Honorable Pailag enter!

PAILAG. No! I know my turn.

SOOR. Let all three of us enter at once, shall we... *(All three enter at once and walk to the table.)*

PAILAG. Let's not waste time about the seating too, please... *(They sit.)*

SOOR. *(To* **OKSEN.***)* I believe you have been informed that legal representation is not acceptable in marital cases.

OKSEN. Yes, I will leave. *(Departs, bowing to the magistrates.)*

SOOR. We must prepare the preliminaries. Wait outside for a few moments and come in when you hear the bell. *(***BALTHAZAR** *departs, bowing to the magistrates.)*

PAILAG. *(To* **SOOR.***)* You didn't express your opinion.

SOOR. No, because we were obliged to interrupt the debate.

YERGAT. On such issues one must not pay too much mind to prejudice.

PAILAG. Nonetheless, we should not make decisions on the basis of what others say.

YERGAT. I do not work in a partisan spirit.

PAILAG. Nor do I.

YERGAT. You did not have the right to get angry at me for examining the issue on principle.

PAILAG. But you made such allusions that injured my dignity. You wanted me to believe that I was defending one side blindly.

YERGAT. Not at all. You have severely misunderstood the meaning of my words. I simply said that white wine pairs well with apples, whereas red wine with peaches is more appetizing to the palate.

PAILAG. But you added that those who drink red wine with apples don't have any taste.

SOOR. To me, the truth is always opaque when it comes to matters of taste, so both sides may be right.

(**SALOME** *serves coffee.*)

PAILAG. So I was right to argue that it is childish to deliver verdicts in matters of taste.

YERGAT. No. I will always insist that white wine should not be drunk with peaches.

PAILAG. And I do not cease to argue that I have not the inclination, nor the palate, nor the stomach, to drink white wine with apples.

YERGAT. You are right, but I was trying to convince you that you do not have the right to judge someone else's palate according to your own.

BALTHAZAR. (*From behind the door.*) I think the bell just—

SOOR. No! The preliminaries are not done yet.

(**BALTHAZAR** *goes away.*)

PAILAG. Nor was I obliged to suit my palate to yours.

YERGAT. No doubt. There are as many wines as there are palates.

PAILAG. And as many apples as there are palates.

YERGAT. And the majority...?

PAILAG. The majority is with me.

YERGAT. No.

PAILAG. Yes!

SOOR. Please, close this case.

YERGAT. Brother, where in the world did you hear of eating peaches with white wine?

BALTHAZAR. *(In front of the door.)* Can I come in now?

PAILAG. *(Standing up.)* Why are you rushing? The nation does not pay us a salary for regulating your affairs. We have taken the initiative to come here and examine your case patriotically and altruistically. We are busy people with things to do—we have children to support and clothe. And today we have come here neglecting our own work to examine your marital affair. We are not your servants, understand? We are not your captives, understand? We are not your slaves, understand? You are the one who should be grateful to us, though we don't want your gratitude—we only want to be left freely to do our work. So be patient until we complete the judiciary proceedings and call you in. (**BALTHAZAR** *departs.)* I prefer white wine, brother, is it punishable by law?

YERGAT. Why would it be punishable, my friend?

PAILAG. So what is it you want?

SOOR. Enough! The tribunal is called to order. *(Taking papers out of his pocket.)* There are three petitions on the table. In the first one, Mr. Gibar accuses ol' Balthazar of defamation and demands reparations. Mr. Gibar himself is accused of being Mrs. Balthazar's lover. The second petition is signed by Mrs. Anush, who, being no longer able to bear her husband's frequent beatings and revealing that the last beating broke her arm, pleas for assurance that she shall not be murdered by her husband. The third petition belongs to Mr. Balthazar, who, having found his wife to be immoral, wants a divorce so that he can marry another woman. I think we must give preference to Mrs. Anush's petition, for although it is the second one by date, it is the first in terms of urgency, and according to her, a matter of life and death. *(**SALOME** serves sweets.)*

YERGAT. Yes, you summarized these cases very well.

PAILAG. A briefing that explains everything in detail. A succinct summary!

SOOR. *(Ringing the bell.)* Ol' Balthazar and Madam Anush may come in.

Scene III

Same and **BALTHAZAR***;* **ANUSH** *(left arm bandaged)*

SOOR. Have a seat. Mr. Balthazar, the members of this committee, being also magistrates, wish to hear your justifications regarding your conduct toward your wife—a conduct that runs headlong against the spirit of our age, a conduct that cannot be justified before the civilized world, a conduct that is unbecoming for an honorable man, a conduct that is condemnable to the conscience of every social class, and at last, a conduct that inflicts fear and horror upon everyone. What is your response, Mr. Balthazar?

BALTHAZAR. 'My wife has been found unfaithful—

SOOR. Quiet! *(SALOME serves sherbet.)*

PAILAG. Hold your tongue.

YERGAT. Speak with decorum.

SOOR. What possessed you to beat your wife and break her arm?

BALTHAZAR. 'Her unfaithfulness has been established—

SOOR. You are straying from the issue.

YERGAT. Don't deviate from the issue.

PAILAG. Don't sidestep the issue.

SOOR. And answer only the questions that are directed to you.

BALTHAZAR. 'Naturally then, it is necessary for us to separate, and, by law, for you to allow me to get another wife.'

ANUSH. Most honorable gentlemen! I forgive him, I only ask for his assurance that I not find myself at the end of such conduct in the future.

SOOR. How magnanimous!

YERGAT. What a tender sentiment!

PAILAG. What meekness!

SOOR. Yet such exquisite women generally end up in the hands of barbarians. Too bad, Mr. Balthazar! Too bad that you have a wife like this and do not feel yourself fortunate.

BALTHAZAR. *(Aside.)* It will all be fine if I just don't snap.

SOOR. You must provide assurance now; if not, you will never enter this house again.

YERGAT. Yes.

PAILAG. I third this motion.

BALTHAZAR. 'My wife has been found unfaithful in her marital duty—

SOOR. How many times have you been told to not make this matter personal?

YERGAT. Someone bring this man to order.

BALTHAZAR. 'Her unfaithfulness has been established—

PAILAG. It is forbidden to speak on other matters.

BALTHAZAR. 'Naturally—

SOOR. Don't talk.

BALTHAZAR. 'Then—

SOOR. You're finished now.

BALTHAZAR. 'It is necessary for us to separate—

SOOR. I will be forced to resort to extreme measures.

BALTHAZAR. 'Allow me, by law—

SOOR. *(Aggressively ringing the bell.)* Shut up!

BALTHAZAR. 'To get another wife. My wife has been found—

SOOR. A few minutes' adjournment *(The magistrates withdraw.)*

BALTHAZAR. 'Unfaithful in her duty. Her unfaithfulness has been established. Naturally then, it is necessary for us to separate, and for you to allow me to get another wife.'

ANUSH. *(Loudly.)* Oh, oh, oh, help!

SCENE IV

Same and **GIBAR**

SOOR. What is it? What happened?
ANUSH. Ahhh! Ahhh!
PAILAG. What is it, madam?
ANUSH. Ahhh... my heart...
YERGAT. What do you feel, madam?
ANUSH. Ah, ah, ah! My heart...
SOOR. *(Aside.)* She couldn't stand listening to her husband speak anymore, the poor lady, she was about to faint.
ANUSH. Ah, ah! Is there a single hair left that—
SOOR. That...?
PAILAG. A single hair left that... what?
ANUSH. A hair left that... ah!
YERGAT. That... what?
ANUSH. That...
SOOR. Very well, that... what?
ANUSH. That... ah! That...
YERGAT. That which she cannot speak of.
PAILAG. Is there a single hair left... The End.
ANUSH. That, that... he was going to...
SOOR. Going to... what?
ANUSH. Was going to...
SOOR. To what?
ANUSH. To strangle me, ahhh!
GIBAR. How cruel!
PAILAG. How barbaric!
ANUSH. Ahhh, ahhh, ahhh!

YERGAT. Mr. Balthazar, your crime is progressively taking on a more complex and grave form. What right have you to be so savage toward this meek and modest woman? Why do you want to strangle her?

BALTHAZAR. Who wants to strangle her?

SOOR. You.

BALTHAZAR. Me?

PAILAG. Are you going to deny it?

YERGAT. You tried to do it right in front of us.

SOOR. If you wish to brutally cut her to pieces before our very eyes, who knows what things you would do if you were left alone together!

PAILAG. Pity, pity, a thousand pities, Mr. Balthazar.

BALTHAZAR. It's a lie, a lie! I didn't touch her.

ANUSH. Ah! Ah!

BALTHAZAR. *(Aside.)* Good grief, what a hellish woman this is!

ANUSH. Ah! Ah!

SOOR. For heaven's sake, I beg you, Mr. Gibar, please take this poor woman to the other room to relax a little. Don't you see? She can't even sit. I beg you to take care of her a little.

YERGAT. And I ask in the name of mercy that you do not leave her side in case that savage tries attacking her again.

PAILAG. I hope you will take on this trouble for all three of our sakes.

ANUSH. Ah! Ah!

GIBAR. *(Hesitating.)* But... I think—

SOOR. It's not time to waver. Please, be quick. (**GIBAR** *lifts* **ANUSH** *and takes her.)* Close the door!

YERGAT. *(To* **BALTHAZAR**.*)* And you are going to stay right here until we leave, you scoundrel. *(Leaves the room.)*

PAILAG. Don't even think about moving, you brute. *(Leaves the room.)*

SOOR. You will wait for us all to leave, you savage! *(Leaves the room.)*

Scene V

BALTHAZAR

BALTHAZAR. *(Alone.)* There's nothing left to say. Every last door has been closed. I became a scoundrel, a brute, a savage. Why, because I want to separate form an unfaithful wife? But whatever they say, whatever they do, justice will always be mine—it will be revealed, of course, that I neither broke that shameless woman's arm, nor tried to strangle her. I will not despair; I will try to establish that that woman is a fox, a liar, and a wretch. I will try to separate from that snake, no matter how steep the cost. I didn't understand a thing from that lawyer of ours—

Scene VI

Same and **SALOME** *(in kitchen attire)*

SALOME. What? What is it? What's happened?

BALTHAZAR. Nothing.

SALOME. What, nothing? Our neighbors came into the house, into the kitchen, to ask me who fainted. But we didn't hear anything from our kitchen. Who fainted...? It better not be my madam. Where is my madam? Where is she? Why aren't you responding? I want my madam...

BALTHAZAR. Go clear your head of your madam.

SALOME. Where is my madam?

BALTHAZAR. Go do your work, otherwise I will squash you under my foot and take your soul.

SALOME. You can't do a thing.

BALTHAZAR. Go to the kitchen and do your work!

SALOME. No!

BALTHAZAR. *(Loudly.)* Are you going to listen to me or not?

SALOME. *(Screaming.)* Shame on you! Aren't you ashamed of yourself?

Scene VII

Enter **PAILAG, YERGAT, SOOR, GIBAR,** *and* **ANUSH**

SOOR. What's happened now?

SALOME. Look at the whiteness of the hairs on your head!

PAILAG. What's happened?

SALOME. *(Always to* **BALTHAZAR.***)* I am not an ordinary woman. Use your brain, you shameless— You have a picturesque wife, and you go and rub elbows with other women! Who did you think I am?

YERGAT. What is this now, Mr. Balthazar?

SALOME. There are women and there are *women*, you shameless man. All women are not the same!

SOOR. This is a novelty.

BALTHAZAR. Everyone is out to slander me today. *(To* **SALOME.***)* Who rubbed elbows with you? You wretch!

SALOME. Who do you think? Why did you pinch my arm?

BALTHAZAR. Quiet, you liar! And get out of my house right now. I don't want you here.

SALOME. I'm not going anywhere. I only obey orders from my madam. This happens every day, *every day*. I can't keep silent anymore! 'Salome! I am crazy about you. Salome! I love you so much. Salome! I am going to order you new shoes. Salome! I am going to give you a raise.' I don't want your shoes, and I don't want you either! I leave, I go, but he comes after me and pulls me by my arm. I have bottled it up all this time...

BALTHAZAR. What sort of a game is this?

SALOME. I didn't say anything to anyone, but now that I see you tormenting your poor wife, I can't hold back any longer, you insolent man! *(Departs.)*

Scene VIII

BALTHAZAR, PAILAG, YERGAT, SOOR, GIBAR, *and* **ANUSH**

SOOR. To tell the truth, you didn't seem like the type to fawn over your servant while having a beautiful wife.

PAILAG. Indeed, it's hard to believe.

SOOR. No matter, let's put this behind us and start the hearing. *(Ringing the bell.)* The hearing has commenced. The floor is yours, Gibar.

GIBAR. Mr. Balthazar has spread rumors to the public that have tarnished my honor, and he has tried to make me appear to be an unworthy member of society. Please, ask Mr. Balthazar: When have I ever told him that I love his wife?

BALTHAZAR. *He* was the one who was supposed to tell me that he loves my wife?

SOOR. So, your wife told you?

BALTHAZAR. No!

SOOR. Who told you, then?

BALTHAZAR. We have established that they were making love in a disreputable house.

SOOR. Do you have witnesses? Who saw them making love?

BALTHAZAR. Who saw them?!

SOOR. Yes!

BALTHAZAR. In a *disreputable* house...

SOOR. It is not enough to say disreputable. You need strong evidence to establish the guilt of Mr. Gibar, and we must be persuaded to rule the verdict accordingly.

GIBAR. I ask you to protect my honor and clear this horrible blot on my name. He is free to slander his wife as unfaithful just to marry another woman, and his wife is also able to defend herself. But I will not accept being an instrument in this kind of slander. I demand compensation. He owes me at least three hundred liras, so that I can be cleared from this dirt.

SOOR. What is your answer?

BALTHAZAR. I want to know what business he had with my wife in a disreputable house.

GIBAR. That is slander, too.

SOOR. You must either support your statement or appease Mr. Gibar.

BALTHAZAR. I can't give one piaster.

GIBAR. Then take back your words and ask for forgiveness.

BALTHAZAR. No!

GIBAR. You must know that the honor of others is not your plaything.

BALTHAZAR. Neither is mine.

YERGAT. Don't waste time with empty talk. We have things to do and need to move on. We aren't getting paid to do this, and we need to feed our children too.

PAILAG. Yes, yes! Reconcile quickly and let it be done with.

GIBAR. I demand honor.

BALTHAZAR. I am the one who is demanding honor.

YERGAT. We are running late.

PAILAG. You, kiss his forehead; let him kiss your hand, and let's move on.

BALTHAZAR. 'My wife has been found unfaithful—

SOOR. The case is on Gibar right now.

YERGAT. Gibar is not that kind of man... I've known him since childhood. His father is also a noble man—his name is Mr. Terenik.

PAILAG. You don't say! He's Terenik's son?

YERGAT. Yes.

PAILAG. I know him, they're a noble family. The mother also is of noble descent.

YERGAT. A one-of-a-kind family.

PAILAG. What's your father doing these days? Is he well?

GIBAR. He is well. He sends his regards.

PAILAG. What did he end up doing with his horse?

GIBAR. He still has it.

PAILAG. *(To **YERGAT**.)* You must see his horse! It's amazing! A beautiful horse that could outrun a train. *(To **GIBAR**.)* How old is that horse now?

GIBAR. Almost nine.

PAILAG. Does it trot whenever it walks?

GIBAR. Yes.

PAILAG. It's a little hard to ride, but for your father it is the easiest thing. To be honest, I was always afraid. *(To **SOOR**.)* He jumps forty feet in the air and lands seventy-five feet away. A very good horse. *(To **GIBAR**.)* How much did he get that horse for?

GIBAR. Twenty-five liras.

PAILAG. But if he wanted to sell it today, I think he would get forty liras. Mr. Balthazar, have you seen that horse?

BALTHAZAR. I've seen him. *(Aside.)* Who raised the topic of the damned horse?

PAILAG. How is he?

BALTHAZAR. The horse is good. *(Aside.)* To hell with it.

PAILAG. You should go hunting rabbits on that horse. *(To* **BALTHAZAR.***)* Have you tasted rabbit?

BALTHAZAR. No.

PAILAG. *(To* **YERGAT.***)* They say it's a little tart.

YERGAT. Yes! It's tasteless, but with the right spices, it is good.

SOOR. I've never tried it. Have you tried it, Mr. Yergat?

YERGAT. No, only quail a few times.

GIBAR. Quail is exquisite.

PAILAG. It must be cooked right.

SOOR. Naturally. It needs to be prepared carefully.

YERGAT. *(To* **BALTHAZAR.***)* Let's not waste time, what do you have to say? Are you going to be stubborn in your demands, or are you willing to reconcile and put an end to this case?

GIBAR. I have nothing against his character. I respect him as a good and honorable man, but I still demand that this case be examined and settled according to the law.

SOOR. Mr. Balthazar is a good man, and he also respects you. It seems to me there is a misunderstanding between you.

BALTHAZAR. What misunderstanding? I saw it with my own eyes.

SOOR. Well then, an oversight.

PAILAG. I think they sprinkle a little wine on it as soon as it is finished cooking.

YERGAT. Make peace, make peace, Mr. Balthazar.

GIBAR. Impossible.

SOOR. Please step outside for a bit and leave us alone to confer. *(***GIBAR**, **BALTHAZAR**, *and* **ANUSH** *on their way out.)* The committee asks Mr. Balthazar to behave himself outside and to not attack his wife again. *(They depart.)*

Scene IX

PAILAG, YERGAT, SOOR, *then* **SALOME**

PAILAG. Come on, let's not waste time. Let's at least reap some benefit for not having been able to run our businesses today.

YERGAT. I agree.

SOOR. Quite right.

PAILAG. So let's call Salome and have her fetch us some good brandy, a bit of cured meat, a little cheese, a few olives, a piece of bread, some barbequed fish, and a little—

YERGAT. What more could we want than that?

SOOR. Let's amuse ourselves a little, no?

PAILAG. Yes! It's not as though we have any more work to do today, and our work today already proved quite productive.

YERGAT. I'd say we haven't had such a productive session ever since we were elected as magistrates.

SOOR. First, we attended to Madam Anush's and Gibar's petitions, and brought some justice to light. Now, only Balthazar's indictment remains, which is more important than the first two and which we can turn our focus to while we drink brandy. Not to mention that our appointed sub-committee is busy investigating whether Gibar and Anush really saw each other in that disreputable house. Needless to say, while our course of action will depend on the information provided by the sub-committee, to me Balthazar is simply a slanderer.

YERGAT. He's a worthless man.

PAILAG. In the end, justice will not be lost. I firmly believe this.

SOOR. It's true—lies, injustice, and slander always bring dishonor.

PAILAG. Hand on heart, we are fulfilling our duty conscientiously, and we have done enough work for the day. But to what end? Those who get things done and those who don't are honored all the same in our society.

YERGAT. If all the national assemblies, councils, committees, and so on worked like us, the nation would noticeably progress in a few years. But who out there will recognize our service!

PAILAG. Let us close this topic and call Salome. *(Ringing the bell.)* Salome! Salome! Salome! (**SALOME** *enters.*) Miss Salome, you are a true hostess. Could you bring us some brandy, a little cured meat, a slice of cheese, some—

SALOME. At your service, I will bring it right away. *(Aside.)* Let me take care of their request quickly, so I can be here when our idiot starts scheming again. *(Loudly.)* I'll be back momentarily... *(She departs.)*

PAILAG. Don't be late.

SOOR. Do you want me to read Balthazar's indictment?

TAKOOHI. *(From outside.)* A woman like you ought to be hanged.

MARTHA. *(From outside.)* You ungodly—!

TAKOOHI. *(From outside.)* Liar!

PAILAG. What is this racket?

MARTHA. *(From outside.)* You quarrelsome wretch.

BALTHAZAR. *(From outside.)* What is it? Why are you pulling me? Why are you pulling me around? Let go of my collar!

Scene X

Same with **TAKOOHI**, **MARTHA**, *and* **BALTHAZAR**

TAKOOHI. *(Pulling **BALTHAZAR**'s arm.)* Come on and clear up this mess!
BALTHAZAR. What mess?
SOOR. Why are you yelling, ladies? What do you want?
TAKOOHI. He disturbed the peace of my house, that's why I'm yelling! Don't you dare lie, ol' Balthazar!
MARTHA. *(To **TAKOOHI**.)* Let him tell it the way it is! What right do you have to come knocking at my door and making indecent remarks to me from the street?
TAKOOHI. I'll do what I please! I am going to lose my daughter. Tell me, ol' Balthazar, do you have any intentions of marrying this woman?
BALTHAZAR. Me?
MARTHA. Balthazar, didn't you promise me a year ago that—
BALTHAZAR. Me?
MARTHA. You, yes, you! Why are you hiding it?
BALTHAZAR. You don't mean someone else...?
MARTHA. No, you.
BALTHAZAR. I have no idea.
TAKOOHI. If you have no idea then hurry up and let's go to

my house, because my daughter will faint, she will die.
BALTHAZAR. What does that have to do with me?
TAKOOHI. Who does it have to do with then, if not with you? Go and convince her that the rumors aren't true, that you will uphold the promises you made to her.
BALTHAZAR. What promises?
TAKOOHI. Don't pretend that you don't know. Even Mount Ararat knows that you want to marry my daughter. Hurry up! Let's go. *(Pulling at his arm.)*
PAILAG. What revelations these are!
BALTHAZAR. Marry your daughter?
MARTHA. *(Pulling* **BALTHAZAR***'s arm.)* He is my future husband.

Scene XI

Same with **GIBAR, ANUSH,** *and* **SALOME** *(bringing brandy)*

TAKOOHI. No, he is my future son-in-law.
MARTHA. No, he is my future husband.
BALTHAZAR. What hellish lies are these? Leave me alone! What you're doing is disgraceful!
SOOR. Now we see why he slanders and indicts his innocent wife!
PAILAG. Bravo, Balthazar, Bravo!
BALTHAZAR. Don't believe it! Everything they're saying is a lie. These ladies love each other... whoever protests the immorality of his wife raises a whole army of women against himself, good grief!

TAKOOHI. This is all unnecessary talk—come to my house and save my daughter! Call a doctor if you must, my poor daughter. *(Crying.)* My poor daughter!

MARTHA. I won't let him go; I have given my love to him. He is mine, and God knows that if I see him going to your house, I will not live... I will die *(Crying)*, I will die instantly...

ANUSH. *(Fainting.)* Ah!

SOOR. Ol' Balthazar, you must bring an end to this circus.

TAKOOOHI. *(Sobbing.)* Let's go, my dear son-in-law.

MARTHA. *(Sobbing.)* Don't go, my dear fiancé.

PAILAG. *(To* **BALTHAZAR**.*)* Reassure them and bring this scandal to an end. I drank a glass of brandy, and it's seeping out of my pores.

BALTHAZAR. What they're saying is a lie.

GIBAR. He appears to be a good man on the surface, but he's deceived so many women...

YERGAT. There's no hope left for you to become righteous, ol' Balthazar. Justice cannot be suppressed. Don't try to absolve yourself in vain! You are guilty.

MARTHA. *(Sobbing.)* Why is he guilty? Is it a crime to marry a second time?

TAKOOHI. *(Sobbing.)* Don't waste time, let's go.

BALTHAZAR. Go away! Get out of my face! *(He flees across the stage, and* **MARTHA** *and* **TAKOOHI** *pursue him.)* Nothing like this has ever happened to me! *(Yelling.)* I am not getting married—I don't have time to get married! *(He flees the scene,* **MARTHA** *and* **TAKOOHI** *run after him.)*

GIBAR. *(Quietly to* **ANUSH**.*)* They've performed their parts very well.

ANUSH. *(Quietly to* **GIBAR**.*)* Like first-rate actresses.

*(***BALTHAZAR*** enters the scene, running, with* **MARTHA** *and* **TAKOOHI** *behind him.)*

BALTHAZAR. Save me from these women, they're going to kill me!
SOOR. Ladies, this is too much. Take your case to the tribunal and have your case justly examined according to legalities.
TAKOOHI. Very well. You already know how serious it is to deceive an inexperienced girl.
MARTHA. Of course, they know better than we do how shameful it is to make a woman my age lose her mind.
BALTHAZAR. Oh! Lose her mind...
ANUSH. I am very distressed to have witnessed such a scene. It's made me age half my life in a day!
PAILAG. Don't worry, madam, it will all pass and be forgotten.
ANUSH. It is very distressing for a sensible and honorable woman to see her husband disgraced. *(Running to* **BALTHAZAR** *and embracing him.)* I forgive you. *(Wipes her eyes.)*
SOOR. This is distressing, especially for Anush.
BALTHAZAR. I do not forgive you. You are the cause of all this devilishness.
PAILAG. *(Standing up.)* Everyone, have a seat. I've had a good idea. The tribunal has been adjourned for some time now...
TAKOOHI. But my case...
MARTHA. And what about mine?

PAILAG. You must both present your cases in writing. Rest assured that they will be examined impartially.

TAKOOHI. You promise?

YERGAT. Yes!

MARTHA. We are thankful.

GIBAR. And my case?

PAILAG. You can consider your case complete. It is evident that the opinions of the magistrates are favorable to you. The tribunal is now adjourned.

GIBAR. Allow me to express my thanks for the rectitude with which the honorable committee conducted itself, examined the case, and brought justice to light.

ANUSH. I cannot find the words to express my feelings of gratitude for the firmness and impartiality with which the honorable committee conducted the proceedings and brought to light the innocence of a powerless being. I shall be obliged to you for the rest of my days.

PAILAG. We are thankful for the sentiments you have expressed, and we promise to proceed in the same manner until the end of the proceedings.

BALTHAZAR. What happened to my petition?

SOOR. Your petition will be addressed at the next session.

PAILAG. You didn't allow me give birth to the idea I just conceived. Seeing as we have four men and four women present here, I say that we don't have a good reason not to dance! What do you say?

YERGAT. Marvelous thought!

SOOR. Superb idea!

PAILAG. But don't forget that this dance must not be on the record.

YERGAT. Of course not.

ANUSH. It would be very rude of us to refuse this motion of the honorable committee. I think we ladies are also pleased to accept your invitation.

SOOR. In that case, I appeal to the patriotic sentiments of the ladies' feet, and I request that they accept our invitation.

YERGAT. Who is going to lead the dance?

BALTHAZAR. *(To himself.)* Imagine entrusting your case to these men.

SOOR. Ol' Balthazar makes five of us. He can be a spectator if he wishes.

BALTHAZAR. I want to be neither a spectator nor a dancer. I want my case to be cleared, and for my wife to be punished.

SOOR. Mr. Yergat is a good dancer! He will lead.

*(The dance begins and concludes within ten minutes. During the dance, **GIBAR** intentionally steps on **BALTHAZAR**'s foot, collides into him while he is walking around on the scene, and begs his pardon.)*

BALTHAZAR. *(Occasionally interrupting the dance.)* Who would have thought that a slanderous campaign would be launched against me? Damn that day I married this hellish woman! Why did I need to get married? What does marriage even mean? We got stuck... we got stuck and it's impossible to get out. Now we have to sit and wait—no, it's impossible. To take this woman and stay with her is impossible. If I'm unable to prove... no, I will prove it; and if I cannot prove it, I will change my religion and become Catholic or Protestant. What else can I do? Or I will leave the city and go. Ah, women! Women! I've had enough of you all... I am afraid of you! As soon as I see a woman now, I get the chills. I am afraid... and what about this snake of a woman who says that I made a promise to her daughter? And the other one... the senile one... she's at least fifty and she says I made her lose her mind—good grief! And what about our Lady Salome? Gibar is pulling all the strings, but never mind that. The married man must be patient and must not get discouraged. I will surely establish that there is no need to listen to those women's lies, that they are slanderers, and that they have all assembled to lessen or conceal Anush's guilt. They think they're going to find "mitigating circumstances"—well, let them! Let them do what they want. If justice is not gone from the world, my innocence will surely be proven. And this damned dance isn't even over with yet, so I can't even have a word with them...

(Dance comes to an end, and dancers start swaggering arm in arm.)

TAKOOHI. *(To* **YERGAT.***)* I cannot stay much longer. I accepted the dance for your sake. Please allow me to leave and console my daughter.
YERGAT. You may go. I will lead ol' Balthazar by the arm myself. *(He starts swaggering arm in arm with* **BALTHAZAR.***)*
BALTHAZAR. Patience, there is no other way.
TAKOOHI. Gentlemen! I leave with singular trust in your patriotic sentiments, and with the hope that you will de-

fend the cause of this unfortunate girl.
SOOR. Rest assured. *(***TAKOOHI** *departs.)*
PAILAG. I toast this glass to Mrs. Anush.

(They all drink, except **BALTHAZAR***.)*

YERGAT. Why don't you have a drink, ol' Balthazar? Courtesy dictates that—
SOOR. Not only dictates, but also demands—
YERGAT. That you not reject the glass that toasted to your wife, especially for such a woman by whose grace you have been able to enter into high society—
SALOME. Who taught you how to speak.
YERGAT. Who has brought you praise and glory.
SALOME. Who taught you how to dance.
YERGAT. Who graced you with her education and instruction.
SALOME. Who taught you how to dress.
YERGAT. Who, expelling all the pleasures and amusements that were abundantly available to her by virtue of her beauty, youth, and charm, took on all those sorrows that you subjected her to, and continue to subject her to.
SALOME. Who is white as snow.
YERGAT. Who—
SALOME. White as snow were the shirts that she dressed him in—
YERGAT. Who at last became an invaluable treasure for you; I invite you to drink to her.
BALTHAZAR. I am thankful for all her services and wish for you that your wife serves you the same, but I cannot drink wine. *(Aside.)* Services!

SOOR. Etiquette demands that you drink. What you are doing is affirming your wife's innocence.

PAILAG. I toast this glass to all who are present.

YERGAT. I toast this glass to all who are absent.

ANUSH. I toast this glass to a long life for the members of this honorable committee. *(They drink.)*

SOOR. It's time to leave.

PAILAG. Yes! Let's go.

SOOR. *(To* **BALTHAZAR**.*)* Until you provide assurances, you cannot stay in this house.

YERGAT. And you must leave this minute.

BALTHAZAR. Why? Isn't this my house? What does this house have to do with any of you?

SOOR. I trust you won't provoke us to resort to extreme measures.

ANUSH. I will take back my petition and try to find a way to defend myself against his attacks.

SOOR. Very well. We are leaving now.

Scene XII

BALTHAZAR, ANUSH, MARTHA, *and* **SALOME**

MARTHA. *(Laughing.)* Ha ha ha ha!

BALTHAZAR. Why are you laughing?

SALOME. Ha ha ha ha!

ANUSH. *(Laughing.)* Ha ha ha ha! 'Why are you laughing?'

BALTHAZAR. Shameless people. *(***MARTHA, ANUSH** *and* **SALOME** *laughing together.)* Shameless, insolent, oooh!

SALOME. You think it's so easy to slander a woman, and mock and ridicule her before the world? Go and kiss your wife's hand. Make amends with her, otherwise there will be worse to come! Any man who wants to let his wife go must be prepared to be ridiculed. *(Departs.)*

MARTHA. Farewell ol' Balthazar, 'til next time. *(Departs.)*

BALTHAZAR. Go to hell.

ANUSH. I wish heavenly grace for you and pray that the heavens grant you wisdom so that you gather your wits and realize that you are at a dead end, that your wife is innocent, and that a mental illness has you imagining that I am in love with Gibar.

BALTHAZAR. I do not have a mental illness.

ANUSH. The facts indicate the opposite. *(She leaves.)*

Scene XIII

BALTHAZAR *then* OKSEN

BALTHAZAR. Well, well, well, council shmouncil! Horses, rabbits, quail, white wine, apples, red wine, peaches, wine, brandy, cured meat, dancing, frolicking around... this turned out to be a ball! And *these* people are supposed to examine and settle my case? It's impossible not to lose hope, but hopelessness isn't an option either. They believed in all the devilries, fell for every trick, and considered that justice was served. What kind of justice is this? It doesn't make any sense...

OKSEN. What news?

BALTHAZAR. Good news.

OKSEN. Things went well, then?

BALTHAZAR. Things are well.

OKSEN. What did you gather from the proceedings?

BALTHAZAR. I gathered from the proceedings that we will not be able to go head-to-head against this woman.

OKSEN. Why? Were you unable to establish that your wife has been found unfaithful in her role? And that—

BALTHAZAR. Her unfaithfulness has been established. Consequently, and so on and so forth and what have you...

OKSEN. Then?

BALTHAZAR. Dancing, skipping about, drinking brandy...

OKSEN. I don't understand. I hope you didn't let the wrong words slip from your mouth.

BALTHAZAR. They didn't even give me an opportunity to speak, let alone to have said anything wrong.

OKSEN. Did you offend their dignity?

BALTHAZAR. No.

OKSEN. Did you not act according to my instructions?

BALTHAZAR. I did.

OKSEN. Don't worry then. It's impossible for us to lose this case. The sub-committee also examined the other case today, and I think it will be favorable to us. From what I know, they will report that Gibar was found with Anush in that disreputable house.

BALTHAZAR. Really?

OKSEN. I am waiting for their verdict any minute.

BALTHAZAR. It's like a burden has been lifted from my heart. Ahh, you should have been here and seen all the things that happened...

OKSEN. Like what?

BALTHAZAR. I'll tell you later, for now I'll only say that I started to fear women... every time I saw a woman, it was like someone was pouring cold water on my head.

OKSEN. Patience and perseverance... it isn't easy to win such cases.

Scene XIV

Same and **SOOR**

SOOR. On behalf of the magistrates, I have the honor to inform you that we will be here tomorrow to report the final verdict on your case, which has taken on a new color.

BALTHAZAR. What color did it take?

SOOR. A new color to the one it had before. I cannot say more but be sure that we will uphold justice.

BALTHAZAR. Thank you.

SOOR. The committee's decision was also communicated to your wife—a decision that was made while walking in the street, based on the conclusions of the sub-committee's report. We didn't have the time to inform you in writing, so now you know officially that we will gather here tomorrow.

BALTHAZAR. You are very welcome, a thousand times welcome.

Scene XV

BALTHAZAR *and* **OKSEN**

BALTHAZAR. Justice has now been revealed.
OKSEN. According to our contract then, you owe me fifty more liras, because the verdict will be given tomorrow.
BALTHAZAR. I was a hair away from being sentenced.
OKSEN. I am glad the case is going well. Can you now pay me the second installment of fifty liras?
BALTHAZAR. There's no need for such a hurry. Let's go and entertain ourselves a little.
OKSEN. Let's go, not to entertain ourselves, but to consult on the course that we must take tomorrow. Now about the fifty liras...

Scene XVI

Same and **SALOME**

SALOME. Whatever you say or do is futile. Madam Anush is innocent. Understand?
BALTHAZAR. Shut up, you pest!
SALOME. If you have so much money, you might as well give some away to this man...
BALTHAZAR. I'm giving all my money to this man!
OKSEN. I demand respect here.
BALTHAZAR. Don't pay attention to her, she's crazy.
OKSEN. The fifty liras, please.

BALTHAZAR. You two are suffocating me. Don't worry, you will get your fifty liras.

OKSEN. Thank you. And you are, of course, grateful for having won the case.

SALOME. *We* won the case.

BALTHAZAR. Can I be sure that we won?

OKSEN. Yes! Kindly, please, the fifty liras.

SALOME. Too bad about the money. They've found an idiot, and they're milking and milking him.

OKSEN. You're not giving me an answer about the fifty liras.

BALTHAZAR. What do you want me to say?

OKSEN. If you don't pay me that sum right now, I will exonerate your wife and have you sentenced.

BALTHAZAR. Come, brother, I will give it.

SALOME. Just give him your billfold and get it over with.

END OF ACT II

ACT III

Scene I

GIBAR and BALTHAZAR

GIBAR. I cannot fail to express my surprise and sorrow for your cold reception of me, which has now continued for some time; and being unable to explain your coldness, I keep asking my conscience: "Have I committed a crime to deserve Balthazar's coldness?" and the answer I accept from my conscience is "No."

BALTHAZAR. Your conscience is more shameless than you are, and you are more impudent than your conscience.

GIBAR. Tell me, please! What possesses you to use such rude language with your close friend, who has always tried to strengthen his bonds of friendship with you?

BALTHAZAR. Strengthen... strengthen bonds?! You're insane! Why don't you say loosen bonds? Or break bonds! You traitor!

GIBAR. You are grossly mistaken if you still think I am the mastermind of this supposed crime. It never crosses your mind that justice is going to come to light and bring you shame!

BALTHAZAR. Yes! Justice will surely come to light.

GIBAR. And then you will be convinced that Gibar is innocent.

BALTHAZAR. And then the public will understand that there is no man so guilty as Gibar.

GIBAR. So you think I deserve to be beheaded, do you not?

BALTHAZAR. You are an animal who should be burned

alive.

GIBAR. I am pained to hear that you think like primitive people and that your opinions do not live up to the spirit of enlightenment of our age. Even if I was your wife's lover, ol' Balthazar, I would have no obligation to stomach your words, which offend my dignity. Suppose I did make love to your wife—what would I have done to you for you to attack me personally? You ought to know that the spirit of this age condemns personal attacks. I have respected you personally to this day, and I wish that our friendship should remain unbreakable.

BALTHAZAR. You destroy my home but defend my person!

GIBAR. Who says I destroyed your home? Let's suppose that I do love your wife... I would have done nothing but defend a principle. But it seems this principle opposes your principles. No matter, let principles be at war...

BALTHAZAR. *Principles!*

GIBAR. Yes! It is necessary, ol' Balthazar, it is indispensable in these times to throw ourselves into the flow of progress if we want to live comfortably. The nineteenth century will not burn alive a young man who is compelled by nature to make love to his good friend's wife.

BALTHAZAR. Save these nice words for the magistrates, you worthless man. You lead my wife astray, you mock and ridicule me before the world, you destroy my home, and then you unashamedly say that you are defending a principle!

GIBAR. Yes! And I reveal these reasons to you because of my sympathy, and to persuade you to withdraw your case, in which you have no hope of succeeding. 'Til next time.

Scene II

BALTHAZAR, then **OKSEN**

BALTHAZAR. I'll show you defending principles... I have never seen or heard such shamelessness! If *I* had committed such a crime, God forbid, I would be ashamed to leave the house. Today's youth don't give much thought to this thing called shame; they rob and steal, then enter society even more freely and happily than philanthropists! This is the "spirit of our times" he says...

OKSEN. How does the wind blow?

BALTHAZAR. You already know. The members of the sub-committee will come, examine the case and report to the tribunal, before whom we will be judged.

OKSEN. Very well. Even though we have won the case, there is no need to puff yourself up and speak harshly toward the members of the sub-committee. We need to flatter and placate them with gentle and sweet explanations, and we especially need to appeal to their hearts, not their minds. Those who appeal to the heart do not return empty-handed. So, there is no need to argue any more, it is enough to plead. When the magistrates arrive, immediately kneel before them and cry woefully and sigh and wail and say: 'Gentlemen! I call on your mercy, your conscience, your hearts, and your sense of justice. I beg you to save the honor of my family, to save my life, and do the right thing, my gentlemen, my brothers... have pity, have mercy, have compassion...'

BALTHAZAR. Yes, yes! This will be good—this is a very good idea you've had. It is always good to supplicate.

OKSEN. Try it, then! Let me see how you do...

BALTHAZAR. 'Gentlemen!

OKSEN. Not out of anger like that, but like this: *Gentlemen*... Like this: *Gentlemen*... As if you're begging them, look: *Gentlemen*... Like that, as though you want their compassion: *Gentlemen*...

BALTHAZAR. 'Gentlemen...

OKSEN. Don't raise your voice so coarsely! Use a more delicate and attractive tone, like this: *Gentlemen*...

BALTHAZAR. *'Gentlemen*...

OKSEN. Bravo.

BALTHAZAR. 'I call on...

OKSEN. Prolong *call* and immediately pronounce the on. Don't separate them so much, so that they do not lose their effect.

BALTHAZAR. 'I *call* on...!

OKSEN. Extend your arms.

BALTHAZAR. *(Arms extended.)* '*I call* on your mercy...

OKSEN. Take a pause... a little louder.

BALTHAZAR. 'Your mercy...

OKSEN. Don't hurry! Half a degree louder.

BALTHAZAR. 'Your mercy...

OKSEN. Take a breath! A quarter degree louder.

BALTHAZAR. 'To your heart...

OKSEN. Good... even louder.

BALTHAZAR. 'And to your sense of justice...

OKSEN. On your knees with your arms extended.

BALTHAZAR. *(Kneeling down with arms extended.)* 'I beg...

OKSEN. Flare your nostrils a little...

BALTHAZAR. 'To save the honor of my fam—

OKSEN. *To saaaaave the honor of my family.*
BALTHAZAR. 'To saaaaaaaaaaave the honor of my family...
OKSEN. Your mouth should also stay half open when you aren't speaking. Your nostrils must constantly be flaring...
BALTHAZAR. 'Saaaaa—
OKSEN. Ok, I think that's enough
BALTHAZAR. '—aaaaaave my life.
OKSEN. You must approach the members of the committee very slowly, as though propelled by an invisible force.
BALTHAZAR. 'And do the right thing, gentlemen.'
OKSEN. Good!
BALTHAZAR. 'My brothers.
OKSEN. Prostrate yourself.
BALTHAZAR. 'Have mercy...
OKSEN. Put your head in your hands.
BALTHAZAR. 'Have pity...
OKSEN. Cry a little.
BALTHAZAR. *Hu, hu, hu...* 'Have compassion... *hu, hu, hu...*
OKSEN. You did very well.
BALTHAZAR. I will practice it some more on my own, but it's tiring...
OKSEN. That's because the formalities that one needs to engage to appeal to pity are quite difficult. Many attorneys lose their cases by not taking these matters seriously enough.
BALTHAZAR. Thank you for teaching me. After completing these formalities, we will surely win the case, won't we?
OKSEN. Yes!
BALTHAZAR. Does that senseless woman also know something about these formalities?

OKSEN. I don't think so. Nonetheless, try to put an end to her.

BALTHAZAR. I agree.

OKSEN. I am leaving, ol' Balthazar, and I trust that I will return to good news and accept my third payment of fifty liras.

Scene III

BALTHAZAR

BALTHAZAR. He is a good man, an honest man, but all his talk ends with fifty liras. I will gladly pay that amount, too, just to finally be freed from this woman's clutches, and to defend my honor and not turn out shameful in the eyes of my friends and relatives. Anyway, let me practice this again... *(Kneels down.)* 'Gentlemen—' No... *'Gentlemen...* I call on your mercy *(extends his arms)*, your conscience *(**SOOR, PAILAG**, and **YERGAT** appear in the door)*, your hearts, and your sense of justice, and I beg you to save the honor of my family, to *saaave*—'

Scene IV

BALTHAZAR, SOOR, PAILAG, and
YERGAT

SOOR. Ol' Balthazar...
BALTHAZAR. *(Not hearing.)* '...my life, and do the right thing, my gentlemen—
PAILAG. Balthazar...
BALTHAZAR. You came? You're here? When did you come? I didn't know, I'm sorry! Welcome, welcome. Have a seat. *(They sit.)*
SOOR. Your case—
BALTHAZAR. *(According to his instructions.)* 'Gentlemen, I call on your mercy, your conscience, your hearts, and your sense of justice. I beg you to save the honor of my family, to save my life, and do the right thing, my gentlemen. Have pity! Have mercy!—'
SOOR. Settle down, ol' Balthazar, justice has come to light. The committee will use every means to satisfy your honor and satisfy your desires. Your wife has already been detained by the municipal council.
BALTHAZAR. Thank you very much! My home was destroyed...
PAILAG. Although there are some mitigating circumstances—
BALTHAZAR. I am very grateful, forget about those other things.
YERGAT. The circumstances are that you have tried to deceive a married woman and a young girl.
BALTHAZAR. It's a lie.

PAILAG. Nevertheless, we magistrates will grant you separation from your wife first, and then take up the other case.

BALTHAZAR. The other case is a lie.

SOOR. Your testimony is not sufficient.

YERGAT. You must read our report.

SOOR. It turned out to be an excellent report.

PAILAG. All the fault fell on your wife.

SOOR. Even though we are under no obligation to read you the report, which is addressed to the judicial council, we will read you its conclusion, just to show you how impartially and justly the committee examined the case. *(He reads.)* 'Now, considering the disagreement that has arisen between ol' Balthazar and his wife for various reasons (which the committee redacts), and considering that there is no settlement between ol' Balthazar and his wife due to this disagreement, we have ruled on their separation with the following conditions: Ol' Balthazar is not to enter this house.'

BALTHAZAR. *(Who was kneeling, now stands up.)* What are you saying?

SOOR. *(Continuing.)* Ol' Balthazar will live completely at the disposal of his wife and will pay thirty liras per month to his wife in alimony, so that she can subsist and live by respectable means.

BALTHAZAR. You are giving me this woman back!

SOOR. *(Continuing.)* And there will be a lien against those payments. And in the event that his wife wishes to take her husband back, ol' Balthazar shall have no recourse to oppose.

YERGAT. Do you not like this conclusion?

BALTHAZAR. Is it something to like? You gave me the punishment.

PAILAG. Did you want us to let her die of starvation?

BALTHAZAR. No! But...

SOOR. If your wife comes back one day and kisses your hand and says it was her fault, wouldn't you take her back?

BALTHAZAR. Of course not, she can go to hell...

SOOR. Then you are asking the impossible, Balthazar. Look at me ol' Balthazar, you are not a child, and you need to understand that you cannot divorce from your wife permanently. You two are one flesh—

BALTHAZAR. And what about Gibar?

SOOR. His case does not have an official air. The nation recognizes you and your wife as one flesh, and we cannot separate you permanently.

PAILAG. Therefore, it is necessary for you to receive the committee's verdict gladly and gratefully.

BALTHAZAR. That means I will not be freed from this disaster until I die.

SOOR. As in, from your wife?

BALTHAZAR. Oh, I wish I had broken my leg and hadn't gone to the theater that night! What did I need to go to the damned theater for, anyway? As if it was the last thing missing from my life... Stay at home! Read your Narek,[2] for the love of God!

PAILAG. What were you thinking?

YERGAT. Why didn't you marry a woman that was more your style?

---

2 A reference to St. Gregory of Narek's prayerbook (*The Book of Lamentations*), which was and remains a household book for many Armenians.

BALTHAZAR. Oh, what a sin it is to get married... my goodness! But whatever the case may be, I cannot accept your verdict.

SOOR. We will force you to accept it.

YERGAT. If it's necessary, we will even put you in jail...

PAILAG. We cannot act against the traditions of our forefathers. You are her lawful husband; you can only separate temporarily.

SOOR. Let's leave then, our work here is done. It is up to the judicial council to pronounce the verdict and enforce it, if necessary.

Scene V

Same and **ANUSH**

ANUSH. *(Her face bleached more than usual, her eyebrows blackened and thickened, wearing a wig, and pronouncing her words as if her two front teeth had fallen out.)* Wait, gentlemen, an innocent woman is being sacrificed for my sake... I was the one coming out of the house with Gibar, not ol' Balthazar's wife.

SOOR. Was it you?

ANUSH. It was me.

PAILAG. Notice how much she looks like Anush. She is a little paler, and her eyebrows are a little blacker and thicker.

YERGAT. That's right. You would think they were twins. This one's voice is thicker, and she has a lisp.

BALTHAZAR. No, no! This was not her. It was my wife.

SOOR. Justice has been revealed at last!

YERGAT. It's a good thing we didn't send the report.

ANUSH. Please, spare that woman her honor, and free her from that ruthless man, that brute!

BALTHAZAR. What kind of talk is this?

ANUSH. I know you, just like I know about your loyalty in marriage.

YERGAT. What is she talking about, ol' Balthazar?

BALTHAZAR. Don't believe her, it's a lie...

ANUSH. He knows me very well.

BALTHAZAR. This is the first time I'm seeing her!

ANUSH. But I can establish that you tried to seduce me as well, and that you are the cause of my misery. You cruel man! You want to present yourself as pious and naïve, but you can't fool me like you can the others. Look at the red mark on my right arm, gentlemen! *(They look and see the red mark.)*

SOOR. I am going to tear up this report.

YERGAT. What a fraud this man turned out to be.

ANUSH. Oh! Pity his poor wife, his virtuous wife!

PAILAG. Let's go, friend, let's go! And you... you get ready to go to jail, you criminal...

YERGAT. To play such games with national authorities will cost you greatly. Everything is clear now.

BALTHAZAR. You won't even let me speak! This is all a scheme, a fraud, and a ruse! I do not know such a woman—these are all the tricks of my wife.

SOOR. Shut up, you bastard! Shut up!

PAILAG. Shut up and walk! You are coming with us, so that we can deliver you to the authorities.

BALTHAZAR. But how can I know that this is not my wife herself? Wait! This... wait! Let me show—

SOOR. Are you still talking? Your wife is at the municipal building. Keep walking!

YERGAT. Not another word. Keep walking!

BALTHAZAR. No.

PAILAG. We will take you by force if you don't come yourself.

BALTHAZAR. You're not even letting me talk to—

ANUSH. Ah! Are you still trying to talk? Surely you are trying to create a new defamation... to slander a woman whose blamelessness is a model for the fair sex! Oh! Most honorable gentlemen, please don't give this man a chance to speak.

PAILAG. Don't try to justify yourself in vain, ol' Balthazar—everything is clear now and justice has come to light and revealed its true face.

BALTHAZAR. Why, oh why, did I need to go to that theater!

ANUSH. If another honest and kind-hearted young man hadn't promised to reach out his hand and show me the way, I would be lost on the road this man led me down so cunningly and deceitfully. Yes! I have great hope that this misery of mine will soon turn into happiness, because Gibar has promised to marry me. I am sure of Gibar's sincerity. I know very well that he loves me, which is why I insist that Mrs. Anush never had an affair with him.

SOOR. Please don't get emotional, Miss. The committee is well aware of ol' Balthazar's conduct and will administer a fitting punishment.

BALTHAZAR. If they make me lose my mind now, I'll have nothing left to lose.

ANUSH. Oh, it's so hard for me to be deceived twice, and should I find that Gibar was deceiving me, that he has given his heart to another, oh! Then there will be nothing else for me to do but to take a gun and—

PAILAG. Calm down, Miss! Calm down...

Scene VI

Same and **GIBAR**

YERGAT. A-ha, Gibar is here.

ANUSH. Please, tell me. Is it true that you are deceiving me?

GIBAR. What sort of a question is that?

ANUSH. That you are in love with Mrs. Anush?

GIBAR. Do you think it's possible for me to separate from you and break my promise? Oh! Please don't ask such a question again unless you want to break my heart. You are my only happiness, you are my hope, you are my soul. How can I reject you? *(He embraces* **ANUSH.***)*

BALTHAZAR. *(With anger.)* What sort of a tribunal is this!

GIBAR. Everything is ready for our wedding in a few days when we will put an end to all the gossip! But what made you come here?

ANUSH. The need to defend an innocent woman's honor. The need to defend Mrs. Anush, whom ol' Balthazar thinks is your lover.

GIBAR. Now I understand. Now I see how ol' Balthazar came to this misconception... he thinks you look like Anush.

ANUSH. Not only does he think I look like her—he insists that I *am* her!

SOOR. Who would give any importance to that man's insistence?

GIBAR. Wait, he really thinks you're Mrs. Anush? Poor man...

BALTHAZAR. You're the poor man.

GIBAR. *(To* **SOOR.***)* I think something is wrong with that man's brain and that you would be doing a favor to society by sending him to the asylum under medical supervision.

BALTHAZAR. I am not insane!

YERGAT. I'm also starting to think that this man has some sort of a mental illness.

PAILAG. Two lines from us, and he would be sent to the asylum. Poor man, what a shame.

BALTHAZAR. Are you all crazy?

SOOR. Let's go outside for a bit, ol' Balthazar.

BALTHAZAR. No, this is my house. I am the owner.

PAILAG. Don't make us resort to extreme measures.

BALTHAZAR. Go ahead.

YERGAT. You must know that an official body can always accomplish its objective, so I invite you to join us of your own free will.

BALTHAZAR. I am not crazy.

SOOR. That's what they all say.

GIBAR. If he's not crazy, then he is evil.

YERGAT. Let's go, ol' Balthazar, let's go. *(Takes* **BALTHAZAR***'s right arm.)*

PAILAG. Let's go, dear boy, let's go! *(Takes* **BALTHAZAR***'s left arm.)*

SOOR. I am glad that ol' Balthazar didn't compel us to resort to force.

BALTHAZAR. Why are you pulling my arms? *(Resists.)* What sort of inhumanity is this?

YERGAT. Ol' Balthazar is a good man. *(Still pulling him.)*

PAILAG. Ol' Balthazar is a prudent man. *(Pulling **BALTHAZAR**'s arm.)*

BALTHAZAR. Let go of my arms. What have I done to you? What tyranny this is... what injustice... what barbarism!

SOOR. The tribunal considers itself very fortunate that ol' Balthazar raises no objections.

BALTHAZAR. You are defending an immoral woman and dragging along a husband who is trying to be honorable. Where are we going? Why are you dragging me? Aren't you ashamed of yourselves?!

YERGAT. One more step.

PAILAG. Walk, brother, let's go!

BALTHAZAR. Don't pull me! I want my lawyer! I will take my lawyer with me, too. My lawyer! *(They depart.)*

Scene VII

ANUSH *and* GIBAR

ANUSH. How did I perform my part? Do you approve?

GIBAR. You were like a first-rate actress.

ANUSH. We must admit that the members of the committee helped us out quite a lot, too.

GIBAR. Yes! It's because I met with each of them a few times beforehand and promised to grease their palms. I did whatever I could to keep your reputation spotless. My efforts were not wasted.

ANUSH. I am much obliged, dear Gibar. Without you, it would have been impossible for me to mask my guilt. I would have been worthy of reproach before the world, and I would have become known as an abominable creature. And who knows what sort of a life I would have suffered, alone and helpless...

GIBAR. There is no need to get upset over imaginary misfortunes. All the dangers have passed, but our work is not yet complete. Go to your room, wash up, show your real face, change your clothes, and wait for me.

ANUSH. I will do as you say. Goodbye for now. *(Departs.)*

Scene VIII

GIBAR

GIBAR. The case is going well for the time being, but things could change if we don't meet our obligation and pay them what we promised... and they are the only ones to whom we can attribute the success of our case. So, let's get to work nullifying Balthazar's efforts.

Scene IX

GIBAR, PAILAG, and BALTHAZAR

PAILAG. In these circumstances, it is necessary to act prudently. The sooner a mistake is corrected, the smaller the damage will be. So, I want to congratulate you for finally recognizing your error and deciding to correct your ways, out of your desire to reconcile with your wife, who is a shining example of virtue among women.

BALTHAZAR. Yes! Yes! *(Aside.)* I know what I must do.

PAILAG. This is how the scandal will be concluded, the gossipers will be silenced, and the committee will count itself lucky to have brought a respectful reconciliation between you and your wife.

GIBAR. When ol' Balthazar first revealed this case to me and sent me to verify it with Mrs. Anush, I conscientiously examined all its details and arrived at the conclusion that the lady was innocent and there had been an oversight. I expressed my conclusion to him, and even went a little further, exhorting him to cast aside the idea of appealing to the tribunal, even if his wife, having been deceived by Satan himself, had committed the crime she was charged with. Ol' Balthazar determined that my exhortations (which were repeated by his wife) were unnatural.

BALTHAZAR. Gibar has a point. *(Aside.)* Criminal, brute.

GIBAR. I knew this because when a husband accuses his wife of being disgraceful, he does nothing but invite the public to take the side of the lady.

PAILAG. What you say is very true.

GIBAR. An honorable man, however, will look the other way to defend the honor of his home, even if he did find a slight fault in his wife.

BALTHAZAR. That's how it is.

PAILAG. To maintain his honor, a man must accept small disgraces.

GIBAR. If it were necessary to behave in such a way with a woman who was found to be at fault, how much more circumspect would one need to be to a woman in whose face is reflected modesty and innocence. You made a big mistake, ol' Balthazar, in accusing your wife and your close friend who *nourished* you with his faith and sympathy.

PAILAG. The committee will pay most careful attention to that point and prepare such a report in which that mistake will be addressed in a respectable manner: All offended minds will be put at ease, and it will be as clear as day that ol' Balthazar is innocent, that his wife is innocent, and that you are also innocent.

BALTHAZAR. How?

PAILAG. It will simply be written in the report that ol' Balthazar had reason to be mistaken, thinking that his wife was another woman who resembled her—indeed, who resembled her so much it was necessary to look at her closely to be able to tell them apart.

GIBAR. Only a report composed in this way can restore a tarnished honor.

PAILAG. And to make it as though the past never occurred.

GIBAR. Yes! Simply an oversight.

PAILAG. Yes, a complete oversight!

GIBAR. More than an oversight, in fact.

PAILAG. And what respectable man can blame ol' Balthazar for such an oversight?

GIBAR. No one, for man is prone to err.

PAILAG. Above all, everyone will see again how fervent ol' Balthazar is about his honor.

GIBAR. No doubt. *(Aside.)* Let's go and get the presents and find a way to pay Takoohi and Martha what we owe them. *(Departs.)*

PAILAG. Which will make him even more honorable.

BALTHAZAR. I am very thankful. *(Aside.)* One must reconcile on the surface and find another way out of this hell.

PAILAG. And you will live so happily together, and more in love than before, that people are going to be envious of you. Sometimes, in marriage, small fights serve to make the heart grow fonder. Be grateful for this small dispute.

Scene X

Same, with **YERGAT** *and* **ANUSH**

YERGAT. At last, a mistake founded on an oversight has been corrected to the great satisfaction of the committee. An enamored couple who were separated from each other because of an oversight have come to reunite.

ANUSH. Please, do not talk about reuniting. I have vowed to live alone hereafter.

PAILAG. *(To* **BALTHAZAR.***)* Go on, then! Ask.

YERGAT. You were not made to be left alone, madam!

ANUSH. Nor was I made to live with this sort of man, who looks for opportunities every minute to defame his wife and make her an object of ridicule before the world. Ah! I am not used to being locked up in the municipal building and suffering the advances of everyone who enters. *(Sobs.)*

BALTHAZAR. *(Aside.)* Oh, oh, oh! Others have made advances, too... rejoice, Balthazar!

ANUSH. *(Sobbing.)* One of them was pulling my dress, another one was pinching me; one was winking his eye, and another was blowing kisses. Am I accustomed to such disgraces?

YERGAT. Don't cry, noble lady. That was the result of a misunderstanding...

PAILAG. Nor will it happen again.

BALTHAZAR. *(Aside.)* If I wasn't afraid of the asylum...

PAILAG. *(To **BALTHAZAR**.)* Considering that you are the cause of this dismal misunderstanding, we invite you to console your wife and wipe away her tears.

YERGAT. And as quickly as possible, if you don't want to make your way to the asylum.

BALTHAZAR. *(Approaching **ANUSH**.)* Don't cry, wife, don't cry! Dry your tears... I have been the cause of this misunderstanding. You are innocent, I am innocent, and so is Gibar. There was an oversight.

PAILAG. Yes! And the report will comprehensively speak to this point.

YERGAT. Try and forget the past, madam!

ANUSH. Can you assure me that he will not find himself making such an oversight again?

PAILAG. Yes! We assure you.

BALTHAZAR. *(Aside.)* Not that I intend to live with her...

ANUSH. I will obey your wishes.

PAILAG. Well done, Mrs. Anush, for abiding by the law and for assisting us with our delicate job.

YERGAT. Go to your rooms and get some rest; this has been very emotional. *(***ANUSH** *departs.)*

PAILAG. *(To* **BALTHAZAR***.)* And from now on, try to satisfy your wife! She is a gem. *(Departs.)*

YERGAT. *(To* **BALTHAZAR***.)* I wish you love and harmony, ol' Balthazar. *(Departs.)*

Scene XI

BALTHAZAR

BALTHAZAR. This is the way of the world. They would force me into the asylum... good luck making them believe you're not insane *after* you've been admitted. If I hadn't said a word to reconcile, I would have been in with the lunatics by now. I am at last convinced that it is impossible to separate from this dishonorable woman, but since it is also impossible for me to live dishonorably, I will restrain myself a little more, get my affairs in order, and someday I'll escape to America... there's no other way. I pity those who have a wife like mine, Lord have mercy on them! Law and justice were on my side, and I still couldn't salvage the case; it is enough to make me lose my mind or even break me. With a single oversight, they wrought all these unbearable injustices. "This is my wife," I tell them, and they're not ashamed to tell me, "The woman you saw only resembles your wife." Explain all you want to someone who does not wish to hear of your rights... what good is it! But no matter—this oversight will now work in my favor, too, so that until I get my affairs in order, at least, I will be able to tell my friends that I mistook my wife for a woman who resembles her. If not for this oversight, I would have been obliged to run away today.

SCENE XII

Same and **OKSEN**

OKSEN. I hope that your case ended favorably, and that shameless woman was punished.
BALTHAZAR. Please keep your mouth clean, my wife is not shameless.
OKSEN. What, then, is a woman who cheats on her husband?
BALTHAZAR. My wife never cheated on me.
OKSEN. Have you gone insane?
BALTHAZAR. Not at all.
OKSEN. Then who was Gibar's lover?
BALTHAZAR. Another woman who resembles my wife so much that they cannot be distinguished without great difficulty.
OKSEN. Impossible.
BALTHAZAR. Yes! I was mistaken in thinking that the woman who was going to marry Gibar in a few days was my wife. I saw the woman.
OKSEN. I don't believe it. A man must be completely insane to believe this. You are free to believe it, though; and now, coming to my fifty liras...

BALTHAZAR. Make it pro-bono so that we do not have to pay it.
OKSEN. I want the full amount as compensation for my hard labor.
BALTHAZAR. When did we agree that I would reconcile with my wife...
OKSEN. Who told you to reconcile?
BALTHAZAR. She is innocent.
OKSEN. So why did you take her to court?
BALTHAZAR. Very well then...
OKSEN. If you do not pay me within the next half hour, prepare to go to court. *(Departs.)*

Scene XIII

BALTHAZAR

BALTHAZAR. Damned woman! You destroyed my home... demolished it. All this expense, all this distress, all this wear on my heart, and only dishonor in return...

Scene XIV

BALTHAZAR, SOOR, TAKOOHI, and MARTHA

SOOR. Why are you screaming and shouting? I am going to sort everything out.
TAKOOHI. He must marry my daughter right now.

MARTHA. Not at all, he promised to take *me*.

BALTHAZAR. These games aren't over yet?

TAKOOHI. You fraud!

MARTHA. You dishonorable man, how can you not be ashamed to have reconciled with your wife?

SOOR. Each of you submit petitions presenting the issues so that we can examine them in detail.

BALTHAZAR. Will I be present, too?

SOOR. Was there any doubt about that?

BALTHAZAR. *(Yelling.)* Get out of here, or I will go and change my religion right now!

Scene XV

Same and **GIBAR**

GIBAR. What is all this noise?

MARTHA. Why did he deceive me? Am I his plaything?

TAKOOHI. Because of him, my daughter is vomiting blood.

MARTHA. And my chest is tight.

GIBAR. It looks like ol' Balthazar has played you both.

BALTHAZAR. I don't know who they are.

MARTHA. You don't know who I am?

TAKOOHI. Liar.

GIBAR. Go away! I will take care of your cases. *(To* **BALTHAZAR**.*)* Pay them off and it will be over.

BALTHAZAR. Why should I pay?

GIBAR. *(Whispers to* **BALTHAZAR**.*)* Do you want to go in and out of court to be judged against these two? It's not worthy of your reputation to have a falling out with them. *(To* **TAKOOHI** *and* **MARTHA**.*)* Go! Go! I handled your cases.

MARTHA. Can I be certain that he is going to marry me?

TAKOOHI. Did he swear on his honor to marry my daughter?

GIBAR. I will try to make sure you both are satisfied. *(***TAKOOHI** *and* **MARTHA** *depart.)*

SOOR. Thank you, Mr. Gibar, for handling this issue. *(Departs.)*

GIBAR. There are other payments that need to be made too, but I will take care of those, ol' Balthazar, don't you worry.

BALTHAZAR. Thank you, thank you for your devotedness. *(Departs.)*

Scene XVI

GIBAR, *then* ANUSH

GIBAR. We are victorious at last! Madam Anush's dignity was defended, and her life has been saved. Now my heart is calm, and I can sleep well at night. It would have been a tremendous burden on my conscience if the unfortunate lady had been sentenced because of me...

ANUSH. I have come to express my gratitude, my dear Gibar, for the courage with which you defended my dignity and my life and saved me from a horrific future. So, allow me to embrace you, as a sign of my gratitude. *(Affectionately embracing.)*

Scene XVII

Same and **BALTHAZAR**

BALTHAZAR. *(In front of the door.)* Again!

GIBAR. What? I thought she was my... fiancé... it was an oversight...

BALTHAZAR. *(Attacking* **GIBAR**.*)* I'll show you oversight! You wrecked my home, and you still have the nerve— *(Threatens to beat* **GIBAR**, *who runs away.)* Is there no end to these oversights? You vile—

ANUSH. Is this appropriate?

BALTHAZAR. *(To* **ANUSH**.*)* And you're not even ashamed of yourself!

ANUSH. Why should I keep it a secret any longer? I love him, all right? I don't want you, I don't love you, I never loved you, and I will never love you—you worthless, uncivilized man. *(Departs in anger.)*

THE END

www.sophenearmenianlibrary.com

SOPHENE

www.ingramcontent.com/pod-product-compliance
Lightning Source LLC
Chambersburg PA
CBHW030307100526
44590CB00012B/554